BLUE RIDGE CHRONICLES

To Judy — Hope you enjoy!

Rex Bowman

BLUE RIDGE CHRONICLES

A DECADE OF DISPATCHES FROM SOUTHWEST VIRGINIA

REX BOWMAN

Charleston   London
History
PRESS

Published by The History Press
Charleston, SC 29403
www.historypress.net

Copyright © 2008 by Rex Bowman
All rights reserved
All stories used with permission of the *Richmond Times-Dispatch*, 1997–2008.
All images courtesy of the *Richmond Times-Dispatch* unless otherwise noted.

Cover design by Marshall Hudson.

First published 2008

Manufactured in the United Kingdom

ISBN 978.1.59629.454.7

Library of Congress Cataloging-in-Publication Data

Bowman, Rex.
Blue Ridge chronicles : a decade of dispatches from southwest Virginia / Rex Bowman.
p. cm.
ISBN 978-1-59629-454-7
1. Virginia, Southwest--History--Anecdotes. 2. Virginia, Southwest--Social life and customs--Anecdotes. 3. Virginia, Southwest--Biography--Anecdotes. 4. Country life--Virginia, Southwest--Anecdotes. I. Title.
F231.9.B69 2008
975.5'7--dc22
                         2008003138

Notice: The information in this book is true and complete to the best of our knowledge. It is offered without guarantee on the part of the author or The History Press. The author and The History Press disclaim all liability in connection with the use of this book.

All rights reserved. No part of this book may be reproduced or transmitted in any form whatsoever without prior written permission from the publisher except in the case of brief quotations embodied in critical articles and reviews.

Contents

Acknowledgements	7
Introduction	9
Haints and Hollers	11
Frontier Town	15
Ambulance #1½	21
Wangle What?	25
Sergeant Major	31
Art for the Dead	35
Star City Star	41
The Camps	45
Crockett	51
Overnight Sensation	55
The Runs	59
Home for Dinner	63
The Redoubt	67
How Goose Pimple Got Its Name	71
Historic Shootout	77
Diet and Exercise	83
Hanging Out	87
Metamorphosis	91
Life and Death of a Motel	95
The Cost of a Dam	99
A Better Maple Syrup	105
Is This Some Sort of a Joke?	109
Not Fade Away	113
Churches of Rock	117

Contents

Soul of the Hero	123
"On the Other Side"	127
"A Very Enjoyable Thing"	133
Where New Year's Is a Blast	137
'Shine Town	141
Old Fiddlers	145
"Gone for a Good While"	149
Pickin' Butter Beans	155
About the Author	159

Acknowledgements

This book could not have come into being without long years of support from my editors and colleagues at the *Richmond Times-Dispatch*. The first thank you must of course go to Tom Kapsidelis, the editor who had the perspicacity to hire me and the wisdom to let me go where I wanted to go and write about what amused and intrigued me. Other editors to be saluted for guiding me in my early years at the newspaper include Pauline Clay, John Hoke, Ed Newland, Tina Eshleman and Mary Anne Pikrone.

My most sincere thanks go to the reporters scattered at one time or another throughout Virginia in the *Times-Dispatch*'s sundry bureaus: Carlos Santos, Bill Geroux, Lawrence Latane, Kiran Krishnamurthy, Jamie Ruff, Calvin Trice, Andy Petkofsky, Kathy Orth, Wes Allison and Paul Bradley. While I was spending leisurely days strolling about small communities like Goose Pimple Junction and Novelty, they were writing stories of murder and mayhem and governmental wrongdoing—the kinds of behavior so necessary to fill the pages of a daily newspaper.

Over a long career I've had the opportunity to work with and compete against an amazing number of talented journalists. To name a few: Ron Hansen, Ian Zack, Sean Scully, Mike Hudson, Bryan McKenzie, Dave Mauer, Bob Gibson, Ralph Berrier, Lawrence Hammack, Jeff McCulley, Dan Smith and Evan Wright. Their work has inspired me.

Finally, I'd like to thank my ancestors, who had the good sense to settle in Southwest Virginia, and my wife, Jennifer "Cookie" Bowman, a California girl with a pioneering spirit who agreed to follow me back to the mountains.

Introduction

For more than a decade I've had the privilege of covering Southwest Virginia for the *Richmond Times-Dispatch*, one of Virginia's biggest and best newspapers. (There's an old joke, incidentally, that defines a true Virginian as someone who won't accept anything as a fact unless it's written in the Old Testament or the *Times-Dispatch*.) In my years as the lone reporter in the Roanoke bureau, I've often introduced myself to people as the newspaper's "foreign correspondent," because Southwest Virginia in many respects is so different from the rest of the state, it might as well be another country.

For instance, there's the language. Residents of Virginia's eastern flatlands speak in a pleasant Southern semi-drawl, while those west of the Blue Ridge have a pronounced mountain accent. The farther west you go, into the highlands and the coal fields, the more you're likely to hear the Appalachian dialect, which has its own vocabulary, pronunciation and rules of grammar. It's always beautiful to hear.

There's also the rural-urban divide. While millions of other Virginians live in sprawling suburbs and cities, the folks of Southwest Virginia largely live in small hamlets or little towns, or even on family farms. Excluding Roanoke, there's not a single city of noteworthy size. Life here seems slower, less crowded, more in tune with nature; people here define wealth partly as living close to kin, and they often describe heaven in a way that makes you think of it as a great big family reunion they can't wait to get to. Maybe flatlanders think the same way, but I've never heard them say so. Throw in other differences—after-school soccer in the suburbs vs. hunting and fishing in the mountains; pop music on the radio vs. bluegrass pickin' on the front porch; English and African roots vs. a Scotch-Irish and German family tree—and you can begin to appreciate what a unique western corner Virginia has.

Introduction

I took the job as the Roanoke bureau reporter for the *Times-Dispatch*—begged editors to give it to me, in fact—because I'm a native of the area and love it above all places on earth. My mother, whose family has lived in the rough-and-tumble hills of Floyd County since the early 1700s, nearly gave birth to me on the side of rural Route 8 but managed to drive herself to the hospital in Christiansburg in time to bring me into the world. So the first place I breathed air was in Southwest Virginia. The first home I ever lived in came with chickens in the backyard and cows in the field, and I learned how to fish with a cane pole. In short, my credentials as a Southwest Virginia country boy are second to no one's.

From the beginning of my time at the *Times-Dispatch*, I defined my role this way: I would give readers of the newspaper, the vast majority of whom live in Richmond and the surrounding counties, an idea of what life is like west of the Blue Ridge and south of the Shenandoah Valley. So it was that, over the past decade, I came to write about small communities like St. Paul and Stonebruise, Wangle Junction and Strom, Hillsville and Darwin. I wrote about a junkyard owner who wept when his pet pig died, about a mysterious nineteenth-century artist who carved lollipops on tombstones and about a tiny community perplexed to find itself put on the official state map.

And a funny thing happened. I began to receive phone calls and letters and e-mails from the readers in Richmond I had assumed knew nothing about the area. After I wrote about and photographed the village of Bonny Blue, a Richmond fellow wrote to say he was surprised to open the pages of the newspaper that morning and see a picture of his mother's house. After I wrote about Busthead, another Richmonder called to say he grew up in the community and wondered that I was ever able to find my way there. It turns out that many of the people who live in suburbs and work in cities grew up in Southwest Virginia. They moved away to find jobs, but they said they found delight in seeing their small hometowns mentioned in a big-city newspaper.

And they also said they were tickled to read about other small places so much like the places where they grew up. Maybe you'll be tickled too.

Haints and Hollers

NOVELTY—The cockeyed joker who stuck the name Novelty on this short stretch of country road in Franklin County probably figured curious visitors would show up just to see why the place deserves the name. He probably thought he pulled a fast one.

What's so novel, after all, about a community that consists of a train depot, farmhouses, rolling tobacco fields and log barns? Out beyond the suburban sprawl of Northern Virginia and Richmond, the state's rural terrain was once freckled with such out-of-the-way villages.

But maybe there's something to the 126-year-old name. What other hamlet, after all, can boast that it buried one of its prominent citizens standing up? What other hamlet comes with its own ghost tale, the story of Hainted Holler? (You'll hear more about that later.)

Today, with its heyday behind it, Novelty is a patchwork of hayfields (the bright-leaf tobacco disappeared long ago), thick woods and small homes scattered around an old weathered building that once served as a train depot, post office and general store.

The building sits in the shade of large oak trees at the junction of Novelty Road (state Route 946), Bar Ridge Road and Listening Hill Road. The last road got its name this way: In 1844, a resident named Burwell J. Law owned a train of wagons that he sent to Lynchburg and back, and he would walk up the hill to listen for the return of his wagon train. One day he fell gravely ill, so he told his family that if he died before his wagons returned, they were to bury him standing up so he could continue to listen. He died, and his family followed his instructions. The road has been called Listening Hill Road ever since.

Once upon a time, Franklin & Pittsylvania Railroad trains chugged through Novelty to pick up the mailbag and local farmers' tobacco.

Residents stopped by to chat at the depot, buy a few groceries or pick up their mail. But the trains stopped running during the Great Depression. The tracks were eventually ripped up and the steel rails were used to fence off one of the many small family cemeteries that dot the fields around Novelty. Though the road through Novelty was paved in the 1960s, through traffic was routed to the north on state Route 40.

Today, you can still see farmers on tractors mowing their fields, but the hustle and bustle that surrounded the old train depot have turned to peace and quiet. Which is the way local residents seem to like it.

"Welcome to downtown Novelty," said resident Becky Mushko, later adding, "In Novelty, there are more cows than people."

Mushko and her husband, John, moved to Novelty about six years ago, and she's one of the local residents indirectly working to keep the history of Novelty alive. When she's not teaching English at Ferrum College or tending her two horses or the stray dogs she occasionally adopts, she's a short story writer. Her work is well known in western Virginia because she has won the Sherwood Anderson Short Story Contest three times and the Lonesome Pine Contest five times.

In collections of short stories with titles such as "The Girl Who Raced Mules" and "Where There's a Will," she slips in little bits and pieces of Novelty and the surrounding communities.

For instance, she said, she came up with the story "Miracle of the Concrete Jesus" after seeing the concrete Jesus standing in front of one of

John and Becky Mushko of Novelty. They're standing in front of the building that was once the community's train depot, general store and post office.

the local churches. The story "The Girl Who Raced Mules" is based on her "cousin Pat who stole her daddy's mules on Sunday and raced them along the Pigg River."

And the story "Fixing the Blame" contains a piece of a story neighbor Benny Horsley told her. Horsley's grandfather was a moonshiner who instructed his wife to "shoo up the chickens" if a revenuer dropped by while he was at the moonshine still. The squawking chickens would give him ample warning to high-tail it. One day while working at the still, he heard the chickens clucking in a panic, so he separated himself as far as possible from his moonshine. When he returned home at last, his wife told him there was no revenuer, only a chicken hawk, and he flew into a rage.

"He came up there madder 'n hell," said Horsley, confirming the tale.

Horsley is a road technician who also does odd jobs at the nearby Smith Mountain Lake. He was born in the train depot forty-nine years ago and still lives next to it. When he's not sitting in front of his ham radio in an old log barn he converted into a shed, he puts tractors back together for the fun of it. Horsley remembers walking down the road through Novelty back when it was dirt and kicking stones on his way to nearby Union Hall or Penhook.

"There was a rule of thumb back then," he said. "If you lived in Franklin, you were born in Franklin." Today, he said, people are moving in from all over, many to be close to the lake. He said he misses the old days because "there's people living down this road, and I have no idea who they are."

Tobacco barns on the southern edge of Novelty.

Then there's Hainted Holler. It's a small dell a half mile or so south of the train depot. It used to be a wooded area, but now the timber has been cleared and the hollow holds a pond. Dorothy Cundiff lives nearby, and she knows all about the ghost story associated with it.

Back in the 1860s, she said, a man named Jesse Chandler was trying to chop down a tree in the hollow. Six times he tried to fell the tree, but each time he would start chopping, he was called back to his house. On the seventh attempt, he succeeded in chopping it down. But the tree fell on him and killed him. Immediately after, neighbors began seeing Chandler's ghost walking through the hollow. The ghost, or haint, carried an axe on its shoulder. For decades residents reported seeing white "aspirations," Cundiff said, and even a ghostly white horse. "You could throw a stone at the horse, and it would go right through."

The ghosts haven't been seen since the 1940s, but people in Novelty still tell the story of Hainted Holler. "My boys would dare each other to spend the night down there, so they'd take the pickup truck and go down," Cundiff said. "But they'd always hear a noise and come back."

And that's a little bit of what life is like in Novelty.

Frontier Town

S T. PAUL—This tiny town was named for one of the saints, but some of its residents are looking for the scoop on its sinners. A group of local high school students is out to catalogue all the rootin', tootin' and late-night shootin' that early in the 1900s plagued St. Paul's legendary "Western Front," a long-gone collection of bordellos and saloons frequented by hard-drinking scufflers who gave the town a reputation for world-class wickedness.

St. Paul might have been the "wickedest little town in the South" in the late 1800s and early 1900s, said Debra Penland, St. Paul High School librarian and coordinator of the project.

Far from trying to hide the Southwest Virginia town's seedy past from the curious high schoolers, older residents seem to be embracing the effort, saying now is as good a time as any to record the history of all the poker playing, dice throwing, whiskey drinking, knife fighting and bare-knuckles brawling that prompted some fathers to keep their daughters off the streets.

"I don't think anyone could ever be proud of this, but it is a part of the town's history, and it is important," said Leroy Hilton Jr., seventy-seven, who spent thirty-seven years as the town's postmaster.

Hilton said the small commercial district along the Clinch River that boasted seventeen saloons in the 1890s was first called the Western Front during World War I: "People said there was more fighting going on in St. Paul than there was on the Western Front in Europe, so that's what it came to be known as."

St. Paul, population 1,007, is a far tamer place today. The one-square-mile community in Wise County still has a downtown, but, like many small downtowns, it has nodded off to sleep. Where once drinkers bellied up to the bar, today the saloons themselves have gone belly up. Long gone, too, are the sidewalks where rowdy patrons were once tossed.

Retired St. Paul postmaster Leroy Hilton Jr. with an old picture of St. Paul's Western Front.

"There are no sit-down beer joints in St. Paul today," Hilton said. "Used to be everybody had one."

"It doesn't really seem like anything exciting could ever have gone on here," said Morgan Rudder, seventeen, one of the six St. Paul students compiling the history. "But when I was younger, my family talked about the Western Front and what went on there. Everybody has heard something about it."

Penland and the students have asked St. Paul residents to share stories, documents and photos of the Western Front. Immediately after publicizing the request in the *Clinch Valley Times*, the local newspaper, the students received four or five calls from residents willing to tell tales, Penland said.

The students, three from an Appalachian history class and three from a technology class, hope to videotape some residents reminiscing about the past, record the voices of others and collect as many photos as possible. Penland hopes to have the multimedia project complete by June 2000.

"Everybody who has called has been real positive," Penland said. "That's great, because most of our students don't know much about the Western Front, and most of the people who lived in the area at that time are getting old, so we need to capture their stories while they remain."

Hilton said the Western Front's wild party began around 1890, when the Norfolk & Western Railroad finished its line to St. Paul, then known as Estonoa (rhymes with Krakatoa). Trains brought transients as well as miners

The buildings in the forefront are the ones that became the juke joints, bars, bordellos, etc.; over two dozen at one time, the businesses had names like The Roost, The Cozy Lunch, Jimmy's and OK Café. *Courtesy of Frank Kilgore.*

This building is the only one left standing along St. Paul's fabled Western Front.

from nearby Kentucky, who landed in town and promptly went on three-day benders, drinking, carousing and gambling from Friday night through Sunday. In 1910, another railroad company, the Clinchfield, Carolina and Ohio, opened its tracks through St. Paul, bringing more visitors and bedlam to the Western Front.

Over the following years, the district grew in size and noise, with restaurants, bars and flophouses lining the street for several blocks. Fights were common, and a police officer once shot a man to death in front of the post office in a dispute over a woman. A government distillery in town labored to keep pace with the local thirst, and during Prohibition, a two-dollar pint of bootleg whiskey was as easy to get as a punch in the jaw.

"There was lots of alcohol, prostitution and wild times," Penland said. "The police didn't even go down there if something happened."

The buildings of the Western Front are almost all gone now. The district exhausted its energy by the late 1950s, businesses closed and the weekend quiet was interrupted only by church bells. St. Paul fell into a hush of respectable commerce. But Rudder and her fellow students hope there are still plenty of people such as Jean Kilgore, an office manager who vividly remembers the Western Front's glory days and wanton ways.

"I used to dance on the tabletops over there," said Kilgore, fifty. "But it was all in fun. I was five or six years old and my dad took me down there.

He loved to go out on Saturday nights. But the liquor sort of flowed freely. All up and down the street there was nothing but bars. I remember, when I was ten or so, a husband caught his wife with another man and slit her throat right there in the bar. It was one wild place."

Ambulance #1 ½

Dugspur—Where do old racecar drivers go when the last lap is run and the checkered flag waves only in the rearview mirror of memory?

In H.L. "Peanut" Turman's case, retirement from racing meant a simple change of vehicles. He gave up fast cars to sit behind the wheel of an ambulance. And the people of Dugspur and surrounding Carroll County are glad for it, because there's a certain measure of comfort, after all, in knowing your ambulance driver has tested his mettle at high speeds and in dangerous conditions.

Turman, soon to be sixty-six years old, was once the young prince of the dirt tracks here in Southwest Virginia, a regular maniac hell-bent for victory lane. And now he's reckoned a backwoods legend. Between 1964 and 1972, he racked up 118 Modified racing wins and 112 Sportsman victories. In that span, his career included 5 Modified championships and 5 Sportsman championships.

"In my day, I was the one to outrun," he recalled recently, gladly warming up to the topic. "After I got to running pretty good, when they'd look up and see me coming, they'd say, 'Oh well, we'll run second today.'"

But for the past thirty-two years, Turman has eschewed oval tracks for the narrow, crooked roads that run through the bent hills of Carroll. All that time, he has driven the ambulance for the Dugspur Rescue Squad, a group of local volunteers who handle emergency calls in the northern end of the rural county. At the Galax Old Fiddler's Convention this month, an announcer drew applause from a large crowd after assuring them that, in case of medical emergency, they were sure to make it to the hospital in time because the ambulance driver on hand was none other than the renowned Turman.

Turman chuckled at the notion of a dirt-track devil turned ambulance driver. "There's a lot of people who seem to feel safe because of it," he said, "but it's not about how fast you go, it's how smooth the ride is."

BLUE RIDGE CHRONICLES

H.L. "Peanut" Turman with his 1937 Chevrolet coupe, which he raced to victory in the 1960s and 1970s. He holds a trading card with his picture on it.

Still, he said, occasionally the skills he picked up on the dusty tracks of Southwest Virginia have stood him well.

Turman's hair has turned gray since his racing days, but he has the same wide grin that, along with his victories, endeared him to race fans in his youth. A giant in good humor, he is small in stature, a circumstance that led to his nickname, "Peanut."

Turman learned to drive on the county's back roads and entered his first race when he was twenty-four. Soon he was racing every Friday, Saturday and Sunday, driving a 1937 Chevy coupe. He traded paint with the likes of Ray Hendrick and other early stars of NASCAR on dirt tracks in Hillsville, Pulaski, Pilot, Stuart, Patrick Springs, Ararat and Rural Retreat.

Turman drove car number 1½, and there's a story behind the fraction. "I added the one-half," he said, "because I showed up at a race once, and there were four of us with cars with number 1. The guy said, 'You boys are gonna have to do something.' So one guy changed his to 111. Another changed his to 21. I changed mine to 1½, and I believe the other guy changed his to 41. So when the race started, there's wasn't a single number 1 car."

The victories soon piled up for Turman, and it was an exciting life for a young man, if dangerous. "Once, in Pulaski, me and Billy Hensley wrecked

A Decade of Dispatches from Southwest Virginia

Former racecar driver H.L. "Peanut" Turman, now an ambulance driver, sits amid the memorabilia of his racing days.

and went over the wall together," Turman laughed. "He tried to put me into the wall, but I wouldn't let up off the throttle. So we got locked up, and I took him over with me. I broke one rib and cracked another one. But yeah, I took him down with me."

Despite the victories, dirt-track racing offered little in the way of financial security. Turman recalled getting paid about $200 for finishing first and maybe $10 after an off-day at the track. So in 1972, he gave it up. "I was financially embarrassed," he said. "Actually, I was broke, but that was just a polite way to say it."

Turman didn't abandon racing completely, though. Throughout the 1970s he worked in NASCAR racing legend David Pearson's pit crew before turning his attention full time to a job in construction. Today, a basement den in Turman's home holds his racing memorabilia, which includes pictures of Turman and his wife, Bonnie, cutting up with racers such as Pearson, Buddy Baker, Cale Yarborough, Ricky Rudd and Donny Allison. His beloved car, the 1937 Chevrolet, sits in a trailer in the wooded backyard.

While racing is in his past, driving the ambulance keeps him behind the wheel. Turman has been faithful to the rescue squad since its inception. In fact, he helped create the fire-and-rescue squad shortly after he quit racing in 1972.

"Used to be, we'd have to get the funeral home to bring a hearse out whenever we'd have a wreck and somebody got hurt," he said. "They'd come and throw 'em on the stretcher, tie 'em down and take 'em to the hospital. Weren't even any attendants."

So for thirty-two years, Turman has hauled the injured to hospitals. He said he knows his reflexes aren't what they used to be, but he's not quite ready to quit. He's still got some driving to do.

Wangle What?

WANGLE JUNCTION—It's difficult to find a place when even the people who live there don't know where it is. Where in the world is Wangle Junction? I posed the question to Walt Lee. "Wangle Junction? Never heard of it," Lee responded as he stepped off his front porch. Lee is a burly man with a bronze-colored tan and a snowy beard. His porch, incidentally, sits in the heart of Wangle Junction, at least according to the aging topographical map I had brought with me.

I pushed the map under Lee's nose to help convince him that, perhaps without knowing it, he is a Wangle Junctionite. After an easygoing trip along bumpy roads, I had showed up unexpectedly in Lee's tree-shaded front yard, deep in the hills of rugged and rural Floyd County, hoping to glimpse what a place called Wangle Junction looks like. The name appears in DeLorme's 1995 *Atlas and Gazetteer of Virginia* and on the U.S. Geological Survey map. You see a name like that, you fall in love with its screwy hum. Wangle Junction. What a hoot.

Lee squinted skeptically at the map's squiggly lines and saw for himself that this quiet patch of Floyd, with its split rail fencing, dirt roads and ancient forests, is indeed labeled Wangle Junction, even though all who live in these hushed Appalachian hills, far from the hubbub of the highway, have apparently always called it Alum Ridge. (The origins of that name are no mystery: the area was once rich with deposits of alum, an ingredient in baking powder.) But you won't find Alum Ridge or Wangle Junction on the official Virginia state map. If Lee lives in Wangle Junction, it was news to him; he said he has no idea how the name came to be on any map or where the name came from.

"I've only lived here six years," he said. "But you know who might know something about it? Linwood Altizer. He lives in that big white house

BLUE RIDGE CHRONICLES

Wangle Junction, in Floyd County.

there." Lee pointed vaguely to the house on the opposite bank of the Laurel Branch, a small creek that glittered in the middle of this bright spring day. "Linwood's in his eighties, so he may have heard the name before. But it's Thursday, so he won't be home. He's got a girlfriend he goes to see on Thursday."

Lee ruminated a bit and suggested I should instead go see John Dickerson, who lives down the road where the dirt ends and the blacktop begins. According to the topographical map, Dickerson's home is also in Wangle Junction. I drove down to Dickerson's.

A puppy frolicked in the green lawn in front of the small home while birds played hide-and-seek in the trees. The crooked creek burbled by one side of the house, and the faint roar of a chainsaw echoed off distant hills. A woman with graying hair opened the door and, after a few wary questions, invited me in off the porch. "There's some reporter here," she announced ahead of me. John Dickerson, wearing overalls, sat at the kitchen table, a giant bowl of chopped cabbage in front of him.

"Wangle Junction?" Dickerson said in a voice that was deep and strong for an eighty-year-old. "I've never heard of it."

John Dickerson, of Wangle Junction, says he's never heard of any place called Wangle Junction.

Dickerson said he had lived here all his life, even back in the days when this stretch of narrow two-lane had a small store and a blacksmith shop. Today, besides the four or five homes scattered across the green slopes, there were only a few sagging sheds and a small herd of cattle grazing on a hillside. Dickerson reminisced about the old days but couldn't remember the place ever being called Wangle Junction.

"There's a woman up the hill here, and she might know," his wife, Wanda, volunteered. "But she's hard of hearing, and she pretends she's not." Her husband said nothing, so she added, in a slightly conspiratorial tone, "He's hard of hearing, too."

The Dickersons consulted for a minute. Neither knew of anyone in the area named Wangle, living or dead, though sundry Dickersons, Akerses and Roots have lived in the area for hundreds of years. The name Wangle Junction was completely alien to them.

John Dickerson suddenly had an idea. "Well, Linwood Altizer might have heard the name. He's eighty-seven. His name's Linwood but he's also known as Kingfish. He might know. But he's not home today. It's Thursday, and he's courting his girl. She's from Christiansburg."

I headed up the dirt road toward Linwood Altizer's farmhouse. Behind the house was a smaller, brick house, and a man stepped out the front door.

He introduced himself as Linwood "Kingfish" Altizer's son, Gene Altizer. He wiped sawdust from his gray, curly hair and explained that he had been at work with his chainsaw, cutting up a tree. He has lived here his entire life, he said, and can remember when there was a small store down the road, though it only sold soda pop and peanuts and closed decades ago, forcing folks to travel two miles up the road to Dulaney's Store, though that closed years ago as well. "Wangle Junction?" he said, looking puzzled. "Never heard of it." He then pointed with his chin to the house of his father, Linwood Altizer. "He might know. But he's not home now. It's Thursday."

Today, at least, the situation was hopeless. I would have to return another day to seek out Linwood Altizer. Which I did. A simple road trip to this little country paradise had sprouted into a small quest to determine why the name Wangle Junction appears on any map. Several days later (Thursday was safely in the distance), I returned to the hills and woods that should be Wangle Junction. The day was warm and the redbuds and dogwoods were blossoming.

And Linwood Altizer was home. He invited me into his fine white farmhouse—something had been cooking—and said he had been expecting me. He wore heavy blue work pants, a flannel shirt and a green cap over his short, gray hair. His brown face, weathered but not wizened, looked like it had seen decades of toil, lean years and fat. His walk was slow and steady. So was his talk.

A Decade of Dispatches from Southwest Virginia

Another view of Wangle Junction.

"There's my sweetie," he said, nodding to a framed photograph of the Christiansburg girlfriend I had heard about. "Most of the time I'm out on Thursdays, we always try to get together and do something."

He sat down in a small chair and his thin, sun-speckled arms reached out for the map I had brought. He tilted it to catch the afternoon sunshine coming through the window, peered through his large glasses and frowned.

He looked for the words Wangle Junction on the map. "Strange to look at," he said. "My eyes are not too good, and those figures are awful small."

While searching for the name, he noted that the dirt road in front of his house has never known much traffic, though a man named Lester opened a store in the shed at the bottom of the hill during the Great Depression.

He found Wangle Junction on the map at last. He mouthed the name and furrowed his brow, seemingly to peer down the deep well of his memory. Did the name ring a bell?

"I've been in here all my life, I'm eighty-seven and the oldest person around here," he said. "I remember back to the '20s. But I never heard nothing of it."

He handed the map back to me and said, "It makes you wonder, don't it?"

Sergeant Major

LEXINGTON—The rumor around Virginia Military Institute is that school Sergeant Major Al Hockaday holds the Marine Corps record for pull-ups. A more graphic yarn has it that, in Vietnam, he killed six enemy soldiers in the pitch dark with nothing but a shovel.

"Man," Hockaday said with a laugh, "that kind of stuff just goes around." Understandably so. The Marine Corps veteran can be an imposing and intimidating figure to the fresh-faced kids who arrive at the military school. With his barrel chest and rigid biceps, Hockaday crosses the campus in brisk, measured strides, his Marine uniform pressed to the snappiest degree of crispness, his belt buckle gleaming, the click of his heels on the sidewalk echoing off the barracks walls. Everything about him screams boot camp drill instructor.

"When you see him standing under one arch, you go under the other arch, because you know he's going to look you over," said cadet Parker Reeves, eighteen, of Roanoke. "The way he walks around, it's like 'another beautiful day in the Corps' to him. But I guess that's what we need around here."

Hockaday, fifty-five, spent thirty years as a Marine, winning two Purple Heart medals for injuries he suffered as a sniper in Vietnam. He was also a drill instructor at the Marines' Officer Candidate School at Quantico. But cadets know little of his past, he said, because his job now is to help them with their lives, not tell stories from his own.

"I think of myself as the sergeant major to the corps of cadets and adviser to the commandant," he said. "What's important now is their lives, not what happened to me thirty years ago. They're the ones who are going to have the problems and obstacles to overcome. I've had a very exciting career, but now it's about them."

Hockaday, who looks ten years younger than he is despite the gray in his mustache, has been VMI's sergeant major for five years. Outside on campus, he eyeballs cadets for sundry infractions; behind the doors of his office, surrounded by his Marine Corps flags and other leatherneck memorabilia, he offers them intimate advice on any conceivable problem.

Cadets say they can count on him for help, and for unfailing encouragement, as they move from freshmen "rats" to VMI graduates.

"In the [cadet] corps, we don't really have a role model to look up to, because people come and go," said cadet Gordon Overby, twenty, of Marriottsville, Maryland. "But I'll always look up to him for what he's done. He's got that hard chest and he walks with pride, and he wants everybody to be that way."

Cadet Kim Herbert, eighteen, of Fairfax and one of the first females at VMI, said Hockaday's size is deceptive. "He's a big guy, but very approachable. I was referred to him because I got into trouble, and he advised me. He was really nice."

VMI's class of 1994 made him an "honorary brother rat," a distinction that Hockaday said choked him up. He never finished college himself. But it was the desire for an education that pushed him toward the Marines, he said.

The year was 1960. Hockaday was sitting with friends one night in front of an abandoned church in Richmond's old Fulton Bottom neighborhood, where he and his twelve brothers and sisters grew up. As they sat and chatted, a Marine in dress blues walked by, his gold buttons gleaming under the lamplight.

"He said, 'You guys realize you could be spending your time better?'" Hockaday recalled.

Days later, Hockaday and his buddies went down to the recruitment station and took a test to enter the Marines. Hockaday figured a stint in the military could pay for college. He later showed up to be sworn in, only to find himself alone. "Where are the rest of the guys?" he asked. The recruiter first swore him in and then answered, "They didn't make it."

Told he would be a cook, Hockaday asked for another assignment, one better suited to his vision of Marines charging up hills and slithering through the underbrush. He was sent into the infantry. He took to the gung-ho, Marine way of life—a life of constant push-ups, pull-ups and other punishments—and forgot about college.

Six years later, he found himself in Vietnam. There, working as a sniper in the jungles, waiting for a target to walk by, he said, he learned patience.

"Being a sniper has its moments of excitement," he said. "But the dull moments are the exciting moments. When you're waiting, just waiting."

A Decade of Dispatches from Southwest Virginia

It was also in Vietnam that he learned a lesson about human resilience. One day, he said, his superiors sent him out with orders to bring back a prisoner. He did. Spying a North Vietnamese soldier laying mines, he shot him in the hip and then began hustling the man back to camp, holding him by the collar. Unknown to Hockaday, the two were now walking through a minefield, and the North Vietnamese soldier suddenly jumped on a nearby mine.

Hockaday awoke from the blast lying on his back, a pool of blood amassing on his shoulder, his left arm apparently gone. "I was lying on top of it," he recalled, "but I didn't know it. When they put me on that stretcher and my arm came out from under my back, that was exciting."

Hockaday pulled another tour of duty in Vietnam and suffered another injury. But between the two tours, he spent two years at Quantico, molding "kids" into Marine officers.

"At Quantico, I was in a position to ensure that the young men and women coming into the Marine Corps would become good leaders," he said. "There's not a lot of difference between the young men and women who walk through Jackson arch [at VMI] and those young men and women who went into the military. They come from every walk of life, from small farms and cities. They're Americans. They're looking for something to challenge them."

Hockaday first came to VMI in 1974, working as a gunnery sergeant in the Marines' ROTC program on campus. He taught cadets about military protocol and procedure, drilling and weaponry. After VMI came other Corps assignments, and he eventually rose to the rank of sergeant major, the highest ranking noncommissioned officer.

He returned to VMI briefly in the mid-1980s but didn't settle in for good until earlier this decade. He and his wife of more than thirty years, Ernestine, bought a home in Rockbridge County, and they opened two boutiques on Main Street in Lexington: the Shenandoah Attic and Victorian Parlor.

Hockaday helps with the businesses, but his joy, he said, is putting on his Marine uniform in the morning and going to VMI to motivate the cadets.

"I'm not in it for the money," he said. "I wish every man and woman in America could wake up and go to work as pleased with themselves as I do every morning. I love my work. When I was in the Marine Corps I loved my work."

Cadet Jochen Dunville, twenty-one, of Roanoke, said Hockaday tries to boost morale and motivate students by the sheer force of his enthusiasm. "He tries to extend that to everybody," Dunville said. "He's extremely professional. He definitely walks with pride."

Art for the Dead

Rural Retreat—Time is running out for any sleuth hoping to unearth the identity of the mysterious Lollipop Carver. Wind, rain and time are slowly but surely erasing the trail he left in the graveyards of Southwest Virginia. Eventually, in a decade or two, perhaps, his life's work will have worn away. "There's nothing that can be done about it," said Roddy Moore, folklorist and director of the Blue Ridge Institute and Museum at Ferrum College.

The Lollipop Carver was one of several tombstone makers who carved fanciful motifs on grave markers primarily for sobersided German settlers early in the nineteenth century, leaving the Lutheran cemeteries of Virginia's mountainous corner dotted with unique monuments that draw curious onlookers even today. Many of the stones stand in church graveyards around Rural Retreat.

"These are the best tombstones in the state," opined Moore.

The artfully carved tombstones are distinctive to Southwest Virginia because of the state's historic immigration pattern. While the English and their African slaves largely settled in the eastern part of the state, the mountains to the west drew German-Swiss and Ulster-Scots lured by companies that sold cheap land in the 1700s.

Moore first catalogued the decorative tombstones thirty years ago. Since then, though, the markers have begun to crumble at an accelerated rate that Moore attributes to acid rain, a pernicious pollutant-laced precipitation that speeds the process of erosion. The traditional Germanic tombstone decorations are a unique piece of Virginia's history that will soon be gone, Moore said.

"As far back as I can remember, they've been crumbling," said ninety-four-year-old Wythe resident Everett Kegley. "I'm not sure it's that acid

This tombstone in the Kimberling cemetery features the Lollipop Carver's trademark lollipop.

A Decade of Dispatches from Southwest Virginia

This tombstone in the Kimberling Lutheran Church Cemetery in Wythe County is the work of the mysterious Lollipop Carver, whose identity has been lost to time.

Blue Ridge Chronicles

Another piece of work from the Lollipop Carver, who provided tombstones for German settlers early in the nineteenth century.

More handiwork from the Lollipop Carver.

rain, but maybe just time. I've looked at all of them. Some were turned over, and others were trying to get turned over."

Moore has identified 160 of the tombstones in the counties of Wythe, Pulaski, Bland, Tazewell and Roanoke that were carved by three artisans in the early 1800s. The only artisan who ever signed any of the tombstones was Laurence Krone, whose origin is a mystery.

The other two tombstone makers are known only as the Zion Carver, so called because many of his tombstones stand in the graveyard at the Zion Lutheran Church in Wythe, and the Lollipop Carver, whose name derives from his propensity to carve figures resembling lollipops on tombstones.

Their tombstones, carved in brown or gray sandstone (once referred to as mountain marble), feature hearts, birds, flowers, stars, wheat, a tree of life and, in the Lollipop Carver's case, a perfect circle atop a long stem. Krone was also known occasionally to include non-German features, such as the Tudor rose and flanking columns.

Most of the three artisans' tombstones can be found in a small number of Lutheran Church cemeteries: St. John's, St. Paul's, Zion and Kimberling, all in Wythe. Others stand in the Sharon Lutheran Church Cemetery in Bland, the Cloyd family cemetery in Pulaski, the Old Tombstone Cemetery in Roanoke, the Central Lutheran Church Cemetery in Tazewell and the McGavock family cemetery in Wythe. The McGavocks, of Ulster-Scot heritage, were some of Krone's non-German customers.

Though many of the tombstones' features have eroded, Moore is exhibiting some of his thirty-year-old photos of the stones at the Blue Ridge Institute so people can see how they once looked.

"These gravestones aren't just historical records," he said, "they're art objects."

Star City Star

ROANOKE—Happy birthday, Mill Mountain Star, and here's your present: federal recognition that you're one of the country's top landmarks.

The radiant neon mega-bauble that shines into bedrooms and boardrooms from high above Roanoke turned fifty years old in 1999, and Roanokers threw a party with fireworks to mark the oddball icon's first half century. Several thousand people gathered downtown to celebrate and gaze at the jumbo ornament, and in the middle of the Thanksgiving Eve hoopla, a state official announced the star has made the august list of U.S. landmarks—the National Register of Historic Places.

Still, national recognition will never match the impassioned local veneration, according to city residents who grew up basking in the star's white glow.

"I remember when it was first lit; I witnessed it," said Jan Wilkins, the city special events coordinator who arranged the giant party. "They were only going to light it once a year, at Christmas, but the people really liked it."

The rest is a story of steadfast love. The 88.5-foot neon star that had been built in 1949 as a promotional gimmick to lure shoppers to Roanoke so enamored residents that the city has kept it burning nearly every night. Young suitors have proposed to their girlfriends at the foot of the star, residents often haul their out-of-town guests up Mill Mountain for a closer look and Roanoke eventually gave itself the nickname "Star City of the South." (Though there is, apparently, no Star City of the North.)

At yesterday's party in unseasonably warm weather, revelers gathered downtown at the corner of Williamson Road and Church Avenue to toast the star, dance to swing music, watch the fireworks display atop Mill Mountain and freely confess their emotional attachment to the two thousand feet of neon tubing shining down on them.

The giant steel and neon star atop Mill Mountain is Roanoke's most well-known landmark. *Courtesy of the Roanoke Valley Convention & Visitors Bureau.*

"I first saw the star in 1951 and I loved it," Nancy Akers, sixty-six, of Roanoke said amid the throng. "I'm from a little town in West Virginia called Welch, so Roanoke was a big city to me. Then I got married and came here in 1957, and of course we honeymooned at the Hotel Roanoke, and the star and the mountain were still beautiful."

Now, she said, she always takes visitors to the top of the eight-hundred-foot mountain to see the star close up.

Residents of bigger, starless cities like Richmond and Norfolk are often befuddled at the affection Roanokers feel for the star. But Roanokers overwhelmingly cherish it and are fond of chatting about it.

Some tell stories of meeting fellow Americans overseas, mentioning their hometown of Roanoke and hearing the question: "Isn't that the city with that big star?" Some admit that when they first moved to Roanoke, they thought the star was tacky or a gross example of bad art; but now they love it and often look up at it through their kitchen windows while doing the dishes. Others recall eagerly looking for the star when returning to Roanoke after four years in college or the military.

"When you see the star, that means you're home," said Gwen Moomaw, eighty-six, of Roanoke. "We've traveled around the world, and when we come back on a plane and the plane comes around and you see the star, everybody on the plane is very excited about it. I have a friend who's a pilot, and he says the [people on the] plane can be very quiet sometimes, until they see that star."

Moomaw's husband, Edward, is the last surviving member of the Roanoke Merchants Association board of directors that decided to build

Visitors stand in front of the star on Mill Mountain and enjoy the view of Roanoke below. *Author's collection.*

the star after World War II. Mr. Moomaw, now ninety-seven, was supposed to be a guest of honor at the fiftieth-anniversary celebration, but ill health kept him home.

Mrs. Moomaw, though, knows well the story of the star's origins. "It happened in a board meeting, and they were talking about what they could do to get more people to come to Roanoke, trying to do whatever to spur the economy. Someone mentioned building a landmark, and from there they came up with a star. No one really knows who came up with it."

In the end, after visiting other cities, such as Chattanooga, Tennessee, to scrutinize their landmarks, the association decided to build a giant star of neon, concrete and steel, visible to aircraft sixty miles away. The association raised $28,000 to pay for construction, and Roanokers gathered on November 23, 1949, Thanksgiving Eve, to see the star light up.

Fifty years later, they're still starry-eyed.

The Camps

STONEGA—You have to talk to the old-timers to know what this former rootin', tootin' coal camp once was like. Today you get a lonesome feeling walking through town, and there's no clue that during the boom years, several thousand people lived and worked in Stonega. But they did.

Stonega (the name rhymes with bodega) is today nothing more than a mile-long strip of small homes on either side of a fraying stretch of blacktop in Wise County. It's quiet in the middle of the day. There are no stores, intersections or traffic lights. The houses, mostly of wood, are crowded together, and the front yards are too small for kids to toss a baseball without breaking a window. Maybe two hundred people live in the community.

Stonega is a leftover from the days when coal companies built and owned whole towns. Two families lived in each house. The rent came out of the miners' paychecks. Everything they bought came from the company store. Company scrip was as common as the dollar bill.

Wise County is trying to find ways to preserve what's left of the coal camps, many of which were built by the Stonega Coke and Coal Co. around the turn of the century: Stonega, Derby, Arno, Osaka, Exeter and Imboden. There are others, like Linden, Pardee and Laurel, which already have disappeared beneath ivy and grass. When the coal ran out, so did the people. Other coal camps, like Dunbar, Toms Creek and Blackwood, still boast a few inhabitants, but like Stonega they're pale shades of their former glory.

County leaders want to stop the decay. They're thinking about declaring the old camps historic districts, but how that might help is unknown. The county has never declared any place a historic district before. Officials fear it might do more harm than good, tying the hands of camp residents who

Scrip issued by the Stonega Coke and Coal Co. in 1939. The scrip was good in any of Stonega's coal camps in Wise County.

want to fix up their homes. Still, it's the only idea they've hit upon so far after half a decade of pondering.

While county leaders scratch their heads over how to hold onto what remains of the coal camps, for now the camps remain most intact in the memory of those born and raised in them.

Take Daisy Lambert, for example. She grew up in Stonega. She's eighty-five now. At the age of fourteen she married the town's taxi driver, who also worked in a coke yard. Her father was the town sheriff back when Stonega had a hospital, theater, barbershop, company store, post office, a couple of churches, two schools and a bustling Polish community. All that's gone now.

"We had our church, a sewing class, a Bible class each week and we were in school," Lambert said, recalling her youth. "We all played together. We had our own theater, ten cents for a movie. Things were hard and wages were low, but I think it was a pretty good life."

Hubert Hylton, a sixty-six-year-old retired miner, remembers his youth in Stonega as fondly as Lambert does. "You weren't rich, but you had enough," he said. "Most of us had to raise a garden and can goods. Everything else we bought at the company store. We had to work, but we was tight. I had to start a fire in the morning and gather coal and kindling in the evening."

Stonega Coke and Coal began building coal camps in Wise at the turn of the century to house the thousands of miners needed to dig coal. The

A Decade of Dispatches from Southwest Virginia

The Stonega Coke and Coal Co. built coal camps like Stonega throughout Virginia, and the families who lived in the camps used company scrip to buy goods at the company store. Whether you worked in the mines or in the store, you worked for the company. *Courtesy of the Southwest Virginia Museum.*

company laid railroad tracks and brought in building supplies on steam engines. The coal camps bustled and boomed up to the 1950s. Then the coal petered out. Stonega Coke and Coal merged with Westmoreland Coal Co. in the 1960s, but that company eventually went under.

The coal camps started dying in the mid-'50s. "Things started going bad, and it didn't take long till the people were out and gone," said Hylton, who now lives in the former coal camp of Derby. "They started tearing those houses down. Or they'd sell them to you for $100."

Pointing to his eight-room house across the street from Derby's only church, Hylton said he bought it in 1972 for $1,800.

Though Hylton and a few hundred others snatched up the houses and stayed in the coal camps, many packed up and headed to big cities up north—Detroit.; Gary, Indiana; Dayton, Ohio. Miners from the Wise coal camps joined miners from the Lee County coal camps, such as Keokee, and ended up working in factories.

Johnny Estridge is a sixty-year-old retired miner who was raised in Inman but now lives in Arno. He recalled taking part in the exodus: "I went into a bar once in Dayton, Ohio, and everybody in there except the bartender was from Keokee."

Not everybody who lives in the former coal camps looks back with fondness on the days when the coal companies controlled everything. Take Bueford McNutt. He lives in the camp of Arno four doors down from the home where he was born seventy-eight years ago. He spent thirty-four years in the mines and thinks people might have forgotten how hard life once was.

"Things was pretty rough in that Depression," he said. "People talk about the good old days, but it was all rough. During summer, there wasn't no

Miners for the Stonega Coke and Coal Co. worked long, hard hours in dangerous conditions, but their children who still live in the coal camps recall close-knit communities and small, company-owned homes full of love. *Courtesy of the Southwest Virginia Museum.*

summer vacation from school. I spent my summers digging the hillside in, planting corn and beans. You didn't have anything. But I had as much as another. I wouldn't want to see those days come back. And if you got hurt in the mines, there wasn't no such thing as workers' compensation back then."

McNutt's father worked in the mines, and McNutt saved his father's last pay stub. In two weeks during 1933, his father loaded thirty-seven cars with coal, earning about $0.70 for each car. From the gross pay of about $26, the coal company took out $1.50 for the gunpowder he needed to blast coal loose from the seam. It took another $0.20 for sharpening his tools, $3.50 for rent, $0.48 for his lamp and so on. By the time the company had taken out its deductions, McNutt's father received $4.86 for his two weeks of labor.

"And we did our grocery shopping at the commissary, or company store," McNutt said, "so they [the coal company] made money off the people. Today a lot of people go to Kingsport, Big Stone Gap and Appalachia to buy things. You've got more to pick from."

Melvin Eads, sixty, was born and raised in Derby, an old coal camp noted for its large houses built of grooved brick tiles. Today Derby is only a row of the homes, some of them abandoned and overgrown with rust and rot, but Eads remembers when the community had a commissary, theater, barbershop, shoeshine room, gas station, school, fire station and two-story hotel.

He also remembers that the coal company took money from the miners' paychecks to fund the local Boy Scout troop and pay the salaries of the doctor and preacher. Still, it wasn't so bad, he said. "We had dances and cakewalks and a movie every Saturday.

"I know we had a good time here—we were in all kinds of trouble. But the superintendent of the mines was judge, jury and executioner. If you did anything wrong, they'd take you up to his office. If you so much as ripped a board off a fence, they'd fix it and make your dad pay for it, take it out of his wages."

Crockett

CROCKETT—The good people of Crockett are stumped, and that takes some doing because, in general, they seem to be fairly clever folks.

But somebody has gone and asked the state Department of Transportation to include Crockett on the official state map, and the state mapmakers said, okay, we'll do it. Now the map has an extra inky speck in Wythe County labeled "Crockett." The big question in this little hamlet is, who put the state up to it?

"We don't have a clue," said longtime Crockett resident Charles Dix.

The spot where Crockett's sauerkraut factory once stood is now thick with tall grass and vines. Long gone, too, are the train depot, the bank, the two funeral homes and the three or four general stores. The church on the hill is boarded up. Crockett today is little more than a bend in the road with small homes scattered around as randomly as raindrops. It's a beautiful place, but just this side of the middle of nowhere, bordering on lonesome.

"We've got nothing," summed up Betty Dix, Charles Dix's wife, as she stood beside the road and surveyed the empty, crumbling buildings around her.

"We don't have anything," echoed Tammy Poston, the assistant postmaster in Crockett, as she took a cigarette break under the hot sun outside the tiny post office. "The closest soda pop machine is five miles away, on Route 21."

In fairness, the people who live in this butterfly- and bumblebee-bedecked village didn't know previous state maps had overlooked Crockett until a reporter told them. But once they recovered from the minor shock of finding that out, they good-naturedly wondered out loud why anyone would bother to put the area on a map anyway.

If travel writers describe out-of-the-way towns as sleepy, you could say Crockett is downright narcoleptic. It's dead quiet except for three things: an old hound dog that barks wearily at all strangers, the occasional Norfolk

Southern train that rumbles through the middle of town and Eddie Reeves. Reeves is a local teenager who climbs onto his loud riding mower every day around noon and drives it down state Route 625 to pick up his mail at the post office. Asked what people do for fun in Crockett, Reeves thought a bit and said, "We hunt and fish, I guess."

The glory days of Crockett have passed.

The post office, which has been delivering mail in Crockett since September 22, 1874, serves 301 households, Poston said. Those families live on a series of ridges and in narrow valleys where winding Routes 625 and 690 cross. Two tinkling streams, Tate's Run and Reed Creek, flow through the area. Grassy meadows and forests, apple orchards and cornfields surround Crockett. The Iron Mountains rise a full day's hike to the south.

Besides the post office, the small homes and a narrow brick building that serves as the community center, Crockett consists of several old, abandoned wooden buildings. One of them used to be Marsh's Store. A railroad car came crashing through the building front many years ago, leaving it to stand and rot precariously. Today the giant, broken building is to Crockett what the leaning tower is to Pisa. "Everybody thinks, why will that not fall?" Betty Dix said. She sounded almost admiring.

People have lived in the Crockett area for about two centuries. According to local lore, the area was called Red Ram for much of the nineteenth century. In 1853, the Virginia & Tennessee Railroad ran steel rails through the village, and, in 1872 a train depot was built.

The depot was the brainchild of James S. "Iron Jim" Crockett, who owned iron mines and forges down in Cripple Creek, on the southeastern edge of Wythe. Iron Jim wanted the depot so he could haul iron bars on wagons from his forges to the railroad. So by the mid-1870s, Red Ram had become Crockett's Depot. That eventually became Crocketts, and by 1925 the name had shrunk to Crockett.

Meanwhile, the village blossomed thanks to a single local crop—cabbage. From just after the Civil War until the late 1940s, Crockett was a cabbage capital. Farmers loaded tons of the vegetable onto the trains, along with sauerkraut made at the local Dix Kraut Factory.

The good times led to a building boom. Near the sauerkraut cannery stood the Bank of Crockett, which was robbed twice, in 1916 and 1936. Down the road were the funeral homes and country stores with names like Huddle-Copenhaver and Hillenberg-Kineer. A hotel opened at the nearby Wyrick Spring and stayed packed with guests.

"People would come here from, gosh, everywhere," said Charles Dix. "People would come and stay the summer and drink the mineral water. It's good for what ails you."

In addition to its tourist trade and cabbage business, Crockett also became the area's biggest market for produce. Local farmers packed trains with potatoes, cattle, apples and peaches, along with onions, hogs and turkeys. The turkeys came from Grayson County, Charles Dix said. Farmers there would drive the turkeys as if they were a herd of cattle, pushing them over the Iron Mountains and into railroad cars in Crockett. The town hummed with commerce.

But the good times didn't last. The iron mines played out. The cabbage market turned from boom to bust. The hotel closed. And by the 1960s the trains no longer stopped. Twilight had come to Crockett.

Today, twenty-five to thirty members of the Crockett Community Club gather once a month to listen to lectures on such topics as horticulture, health and dairy farming, and that's about all the excitement residents need to stay happy, Charles Dix said. Some years back a few fellows from Speedwell brawled on the streets with local lads, and seven years ago the woman who served as postmaster was murdered, but other than those two events no one in Crockett could think of anything out of the ordinary ever happening here.

And that's the way they like it.

"I can't think of living anywhere else," said Betty Dix, who was born in nearby Huckleberry. "We love it here."

So who petitioned the state to put Crockett on the state map? The Virginia Department of Transportation's cartography office said local residents can thank a Towson, Maryland man named—James Crockett.

Reached by telephone, Crockett said, yes, he's the guy. He said Iron Jim Crockett is his great-great-great-great-grandfather. Petitioning Virginia to put the community on the map, he said, was a point of family pride.

"I do a lot of genealogy and family research in Virginia," Crockett said. "I went down there in 1992 and Crockett was on the state map. I went back in 1993 and picked up a state map, and it wasn't on there anymore. I wrote the state and said it should be on the map because Crockett has its own zip code. So if people in Crockett ask who had it put back on the map, you can tell them it was me."

Overnight Sensation

CLINTWOOD—Faye "Wild Granny" Senter, even at the autumnal age of seventy-six, says she is looking now more than ever for that Nashville recording deal that will bring her fame. And—who can say?—maybe she'll succeed. Maybe the songs she has scribbled into notebooks and stuffed into drawers—with titles such as "Somebody Stole the Outhouse," "Take It Easy, Greasy" and "Hang on to Your Bloomers"—have a place in music stores. But Wild Granny is beginning to doubt.

"I'll be seventy-seven next month," she said this week, sitting inside her cinder block house in Clintwood. "I've been trying a long time. I ain't got nowhere yet."

A troubadour who sings of Appalachian troubles in a voice that sometimes creaks like a loose floorboard and sometimes sails like a mellifluous echo over the hills, Wild Granny is an authentic mountain woman.

Her accent makes Loretta Lynn sound like a city slicker; the politics of her music, featuring diatribes against Congress, odes to the working poor and praise for the coal miners' union, make her close kin to Dust Bowl minstrel Woody Guthrie. Her bluegrass ballads are as heavy with sentiment as a Hallmark card but full of quirky revelations about her long, hard life, which she has weathered with a hearty laugh.

"Honey, I've worked in so many factories you wouldn't believe it," she said. "I've made brake shoes, telephones, flamethrowers, parachutes, time bombs, boxes and doughnuts. I've been a maid, opened my own restaurant two times, been a cook, a waitress, a cab driver and a caregiver for the elderly. I've done some living."

It takes a funny woman to croon "I've Been Married Three Times and Never Been Satisfied." Or the crowd-pleasing "Somebody Stole the Outhouse," a fast-paced ditty about a toilet-bereft family that literally has "got nowheres to go."

Faye "Wild Granny" Senter of Clintwood picks out a tune on her guitar while sitting on the front steps of her home.

Wild Granny, you see, is a real cutup. A few years back, for example, when she had her own show on public radio station WMMT in Whitesburg, Kentucky, she said she acted "man crazy" just to cause mischief. She said her family didn't appreciate her hijinks. "They want me to be just granny, not Wild Granny."

And back when her band, the Unknown Hillbillies, performed in Clintwood, she and the other women in the group wore overalls and beards, and once they brought a cardboard outhouse on stage with them.

But success has been elusive for Wild Granny. She's played in North Carolina and Kentucky and in her hometown of Clintwood, but few know her or her unusual music outside Appalachia. A record deal, she said, could change that.

"I've been trying these last fifteen years," she said, "but I guess I've not tried very hard."

Wild Granny's roots are pure bluegrass. Her parents, Ely and Mattie Wallace, moved to Clintwood from Elkhorn City, Kentucky, in a covered wagon before she was born. The third of ten children, she said she grew up listening to her momma sing old-timey country tunes and hillbilly ballads. Wild Granny said she started singing soon after learning to talk, and a cousin taught her to play the guitar. At fourteen, she and a sister won a talent show in Clintwood for singing "Gathering Flowers from the Hillside."

She eventually put away her musical ambitions to take on the chores of life. Like her song says, she married three times. The first man ran off on her, the second one died, and her third husband turned out to be already married. "We lived together for five years before I found out we weren't legally married," she said, chuckling at the scandal of it all.

About fifteen years ago, she took up singing and writing songs. "I smoked for a long time, and when I gave it up, I got my voice back," she explained.

Wild Granny has written about two hundred songs since then, most of them copyrighted. She writes them out in a wobbly hand—she quit school after the eighth grade—and a few of them she typed, using only her index fingers. She went back to longhand when her old typewriter busted.

She formed a string band, the Unknown Hillbillies, with a daughter and two cousins and performed in Clintwood. That's when she took the name Wild Granny and developed her original sound, playing guitar and banjo jingles with cantankerous titles such as "Root Hog or Die" and "You Knock My Poor Heart Out of Shape."

The songs are as odd as the titles. Take, for example, the one called "What's Going to Go Next?," a tune about the accumulating ailments of old age: "Lots of people say when they look at me, She sure don't look like she used to be. What's going to go next? Will it be my heart? My doctor said I was falling apart. My hearing's about gone, will I lose my teeth? There'll be no need to holler 'Where's the beef?'"

Songs like that might look corny on paper, in Wild Granny's rugged spelling, but her voice imbues her words with a defiant cheer. Embellished occasionally with a woeful yodel, her music is to the ear what wild onions are to the tongue—a powerful pleasure that doesn't agree with everyone.

Her band broke up, but the head of the Possum International Tape Club in Kentucky heard Wild Granny play and offered to sponsor her if she performed shows for WMMT. Wild Granny agreed and, in 1995, started doing a thirty-minute weekly show, spinning yarns and singing her songs on the air.

"She did all original stuff, from old-timey to bluegrassy," said WMMT staff member Cheryl Marshall. "It was original and outrageous, and she was outrageous."

Today, the station offers tapes of Wild Granny's music as an inducement to potential donors during fund drives.

Wild Granny spent two years and eight months doing the show but had to quit when her youngest son—one of five children—developed a fatal cancer.

Lately, she's been performing at local nursing homes, dancing around with the elderly residents. She plans to play at a talent show in Kingsport,

Tennessee, today (June 17, 2000) and acknowledges the performance might be her last chance to grab the attention of someone in the recording industry.

"I've kind of slowed down in the last months," she said. "I ran out of vitamins and haven't been feeling well."

Still, she said, she's hopeful. You never can tell when a Nashville scout might be sitting there in the front row listening carefully, with a blank contract and, more importantly, a taste for wild onions.

Note: So far, at least, Wild Granny has not won that recording contract.

The Runs

INDEPENDENCE—Here in this mountain community just above the North Carolina state line, they race outhouses. Not every day, mind you, or even frequently. But once a year during the town's Mountain Foliage Festival, outhouses on wheels become the chariots of huffing and puffing competitors who haul them along Main Street at breakneck speed while hundreds line the sidewalk and cheer.

"It's a pretty neat thing," said Larry Bolt, Grayson County's commissioner of the revenue, who has taken part in the town's Grand Privy Race for the local Republican Party team. "You get to run up and down the street with it. And when the weather's good there are lots of people."

The Grand Privy Race, which took place the morning of October 14, 2006, has been a part of Independence's fall celebration since 1982, with the exception of an eight-year absence between 1986 and 1994.

Now, officials in Independence (population 971) are plotting to expand their popular portable potty pastime from mere local peculiarity to a sport with statewide appeal. They're working to have the town designated Virginia's official privy race site, either by gubernatorial proclamation or by General Assembly resolution.

No other communities are vying for the honor.

In a larger context, the move is just the latest ploy by a small town to lure tourists to Southwest Virginia. In the past decade, as textile and furniture factories have closed, highland communities have worked to boost tourism by promoting their bluegrass music, mountain crafts and scenic beauty. Independence's resolve to put its latrine racing in the limelight is a twist on the tourism theme.

In practical terms, officials hope a state sanction will not only swell the crowd size at the annual two-day festival but also boost the number of competitors, drawing six-person teams from across the commonwealth willing to pull a one-hundred-pound toilet more than a tenth of a mile. Last year, the field of teams in the double-elimination event shrank to six, a cause of concern for a town that hopes to call itself the state capital of perambulant water closets.

"We're trying to really push getting people here," admitted Carol Lundgren, treasurer of the town's special events committee. The town created the committee several years ago to breathe life into the outhouse race. One of the committee's first acts was to pair the dash with a Potty Princess Pageant, the first of which was won by a grown man wearing a pink negligee and a diaper, Lundgren recalled. ("Why not?" she explained.)

She added that the race already has started to attract teams from outside Independence. Last year, she said, a U.S. Coast Guard team from Newport News joined the johnny-house sprint, and for the first time ever, the prize trophy—a miniature outhouse, naturally—went to an out-of-town competitor, a corporate-sponsored team from nearby Galax.

Terry Anderson, a forty-eight-year-old workingman who said he has pulled outhouses in the competition off and on for twenty years, said to see the race once is to become a lifetime fan. The local rivalries, such as Republicans vs. Democrats and Dutch-Mundy Chevrolet vs. the now-defunct Food Bonanza, can bring the crowd to a cheering frenzy.

"Once, at Vaughan-Bassett Furniture, we built an outhouse out of oak," Anderson recalled as he sat on a barstool in Ogle's Deli and nursed a beer. "It must have weighed six hundred pounds. Nautilus [Inc.] had something made out of fiberglass that looked like it weighed fifty pounds. And we beat 'em. I do take pride in that."

Most of the racers are simple constructions: an outhouse sitting atop two bicycles welded together, for instance. The rules state that teams can consist of four pullers in front and one brakeman behind, or three pullers and two brakemen. But the rules require that each outhouse has a sixth team member sitting in the outhouse, and the outhouses can have no doors—"to give the public full viewing pleasure of the kings or queens on their thrones." At various points in the race, teams have to stop and members have to rotate positions, a rule that forces teams not only to be fleet but coordinated as well. Occasionally, outhouses topple over and occupants tumble out.

To give the race wider appeal, the town is working with state Delegate Bill Carrico Sr., Republican from Grayson, to have Independence declared the state's official privy race site. Carrico said he's waiting for the town to present him with some research on outhouse racing in general before deciding whether to ask the governor for a proclamation or take the matter to the General Assembly.

In the meantime, the town is fairly confident it already is Virginia's outhouse racing capital, and any community that makes a rival claim is just a pretender to the throne. Or, if you will, a johnny-come-lately.

Home for Dinner

ROANOKE—Drifters, drinkers, hobos and bums, along with senators, sportswriters and stockbrokers, have sat shoulder to shoulder on the stools of the Texas Tavern since the Great Depression, and that makes the diner one of this city's most enduring and endearing fixtures.

The diner turned seventy on February 13, 2000, and in the seven decades that Texas Tavern cooks have served up chili and hot dogs, Roanokers have seen fancier restaurants come and go. Some disappeared almost as rapidly as the stingy portions of haute cuisine they served. The gas stations, hotels and the movie theater that once shared the downtown with the Texas Tavern also vanished long ago. But through the Depression, the advent of fast-food culture and the modern exodus of downtown businesses to suburban malls, the tiny Texas Tavern has survived. The twenty-four-hour-a-day eatery, no bigger than the average room at a Ramada Inn, has put steaming cups of coffee into the hands of both the down-and-out and the up-and-coming.

Lawyers stop by in the afternoon for a bite on their way to court. Barflies wobble in at midnight to add ballast to their stomachs. Brawlers occasionally drop by in the dim hours of the morning to study the bloodstains on their shirts. Police officers walking the beat come in to thaw out.

"At times, you can go in there and see people in tuxedos sitting next to people just out of the Roanoke City Jail," said Delegate Clifton A. Woodrum, a Roanoke Democrat and patron of the Texas Tavern. "It's Roanoke's melting pot."

"He hit the nail on the head," said the diner's owner, Jim Bullington. "I walked out to the counter one day and there was a judge sitting there talking to a fellow who looked down on his luck. The judge left, and the fellow said, 'I just got out of jail, and that judge was the guy who put me in.'"

The Texas Tavern in Roanoke has served chili and hot dogs for decades. Mustard, not ketchup, is the preferred condiment.

The Texas Tavern earned a little spotlight in Richmond recently when the General Assembly passed a resolution commending the diner for "offering the finest in Southwest Virginia cuisine [to] young and old; rich and poor; blue collar, white collar and no collar." Woodrum sponsored the seventieth birthday resolution, which also says, "The loyalty of its customers, the lines that frequently snake around the block, and the patrons at 4 a.m. all attest to the enduring popularity of a Roanoke institution."

The Texas Tavern, at 114 Church Avenue, has just ten stools, and it has made the most of them. As its slogan says, the diner serves "One thousand customers, ten at a time." Another slogan framed on the wall says, "We don't cash checks or play with bumblebees."

Other frames behind the counter contain an ad for bail bonds and a promise that patrons who don't get a receipt will get five dollars instead. The big neon arrow hanging outside the diner isn't subtle: it says "EAT."

Napkin dispensers and salt-and-pepper shakers with dented metal lids line the metal counter, along with bottles of mustard. One of the diner's rules is that only children younger than twelve can get ketchup. "We maintain that ketchup was invented to put on French fries, not hamburgers," Bullington said. "We don't serve French fries." Or any other vegetable.

A Decade of Dispatches from Southwest Virginia

A rare slow day in the Texas Tavern. Occasionally customers have to line up outside the door.

A long metal pipe runs along the bottom of the counter and serves as a footrest. The pipe is full of holes, a testament to the erosive powers of shoe leather.

Thousands of patrons over the years have sat on the stools and chewed hamburgers and hot dogs, gabbed with the affable cooks and downed bowl after bowl of chili. The diner's specialty is the Cheesy Western, a burger with egg, cheese, relish and, if you want, onion.

"Back in high school, after dropping off your date, you'd go in there and meet the guys," said Eric Fitzpatrick, a local artist who frequents the diner and has painted it. "I'd get a 'bowl with' and a Nehi grape. It's a great place." A "bowl with" is Texas Tavern shorthand for chili with onions.

"I remember one time when I was a kid, I finished swimming at the YMCA, and before the bus came, I went into the Texas Tavern and had five bowls of chili," Woodrum recalled. "The chili is great, but that's the day I swore off it. I've been a Cheesy Western man ever since."

Bullington estimated that, on a typical weekend night, the cooks serve forty gallons of chili, six hundred burgers and five hundred hot dogs. Though the diner has but ten stools, at times more than fifty customers have packed into the narrow space.

Bullington is the grandson of the diner's founder, Isaac N. Bullington. The grandson said the eatery got started this way: Isaac Bullington was an advance man for the Ringling Bros. and Barnum & Bailey Circus during the 1920s. One day while in San Antonio, he ate a bowl of chili at a local hotel. He liked the chili so much he slipped the chef some money for the recipe and then opened a restaurant in Roanoke. He named it the Texas Tavern in honor of the chili's birthplace.

Bullington said he takes pleasure in outlasting bigger, trendier restaurants. "You've got to have a product that customers like," he said. "You've got to have good and loyal employees, and good and loyal customers. Here, we know the majority of our customers by name, and they know us by name. When you come here, it's like going over to family's house for dinner."

Especially if your family serves nothing but burgers, hot dogs and bowls of chili and encourages anyone to wander in off the street.

Fitzpatrick, like Woodrum, said he loves the diner's democratic atmosphere. "There is no stereotype that you can use to describe the customers. Every walk of life comes into the Texas Tavern."

The Redoubt

STROM—To the road-weary traveler, the community of Strom, with its mountain breezes, tinkling creeks and shady trees, seems a refreshing piece of paradise. But that's not necessarily the way Melinda Persinger sees it. Persinger lives in Strom and spends much of her days sitting behind the counter of the little country store she owns, the Roaring Run Grocery. The store is at the very heart of this quiet community in Botetourt County, and Persinger is the most delightfully bored storekeeper you're ever likely to meet. She reads books while waiting for customers to show up in this out-of-the-way corner of Virginia, and some days customers are few and far between. You can read a lot on days like that, she's found.

Ask her if she owns the store and she'll roll her eyes and wearily sigh, "Yeah," as if the fates have cursed her with an unwanted labor. Tell her it's a fine-looking, old-fashioned store and she'll immediately perk up with a question: "Know anybody who wants to buy it?"

Persinger, forty-two, is a Baltimore native, a big-city girl who married a Marine from Delaware. They decided nine years ago to move to Strom, where his dad grew up. So here they are.

As it turns out, one person's hushed paradise is just a country storekeeper's long, long day.

Strom sits on state Route 615, which is a Virginia Scenic Byway, a designation given only to the state's prettiest stretches of roads, and 615 deserves it. The road meanders along Craig Creek and through Strom, which really includes nothing but Persinger's store, a campground and a dozen or so scattered houses, where the waters of the aptly named Roaring Run rush into the Craig.

Route 615 runs through the George Washington and Jefferson National Forests. Deisher Mountain rises up in the west. The place is a mecca for hunters and those who love to fish (the Roaring Run is stocked with trout),

BLUE RIDGE CHRONICLES

Melinda Persinger owns the Roaring Run Grocery in the community of Strom.

and outdoor lovers come from all over on summer weekends to camp by the creek and hike through the woods.

Persinger said she might see a few dozen customers on any weekday, but hundreds on weekends. One of the customers this week was Lisa Kirkwood, who brought her son and daughter from their home in Bedford County to enjoy the fresh air of Strom.

"I love it here," Kirkwood said. "We camped down here when I was little, that's the only way I know the place is here. I drove an hour and fifteen minutes just to get here today. My son can play in the creek and I can just lie on the bank and read."

Persinger sees quite a few customers like Kirkwood, people who love nature and the outdoors and, like the self-reliant residents of Strom, think it's a great place to experience all of it. Her store caters to that clientele. In addition to snacks, chips and beer, she also sells muzzleloading supplies, charcoal briquettes, blaze-orange hunting caps, rolling papers, license plates featuring the Confederate battle flag and BC Powder. The magazine rack on the wall paints a good picture of the customers who wander in from the heat. The magazines include *Field & Stream*, *Cabela's Outfitter Journal*, *Popular Mechanics*, *Family Handyman* and *Peterson's Hunting*.

A Decade of Dispatches from Southwest Virginia

The Roaring Run Grocery sits in Strom at the confluence of two streams, the Roaring Run and Craig Creek.

Visitors from all over come to Strom to splash in the waters of the Roaring Run.

Persinger also fixes lunches for customers. The menu includes egg sandwiches and the perennial favorite, bologna and cheese.

The little country store is a great reason that people stop off in Strom, where life is slow, slow, slow. Persinger makes sure the store has what people around here need to keep enjoying the peaceful scenery and isolation.

"Yeah, everybody who's here, this is where they want to be, and they wouldn't want to be anywhere else," Persinger said.

How Goose Pimple Got Its Name

GOOSE PIMPLE JUNCTION—James Gilmer, whom it's not unusual to find with engine oil on his hands, was born and raised in Goose Pimple Junction, and he has seen the changes close up. He's sixty years old.

"It's a quiet little community," the farmer, trucker and part-time tinker says as he looks at the grassy hill across the road from his small house. "Nothing goes on that I know of. Nothing exciting ever goes on." But that wasn't always the case. Nowadays, the only noise you're likely to hear in this Washington County hamlet is the barking of dogs, the passing of trucks and the whir of a lawnmower. But once, the racket of feuding neighbors was so pronounced that it led residents to give the place its name. So the story goes, anyway.

Located about three miles east of Bristol and a quarter-mile north of the Tennessee line, Goose Pimple Junction sits among the rolling hills and tilted hayfields of Appalachia. Small barns and cattle dot the landscape. The center of the community is a junction where the Old Jonesboro Road, a former stagecoach route, runs straight into a hard elbow of state Route 649. The community's brick church, Beulah Land Baptist, sits at the corner of Old Jonesboro and a tiny road called Castle Yonder Lane. A faded roadside sign says Goose Pimple Junction's population is 154, but the sign hasn't been updated since 1974.

Gilmer, pulling a tobacco pouch from his overalls, says he grew up on a farm in Goose Pimple Junction on a twist of the road not far from where he now lives. His daddy was a sharecropper, and so was his granddaddy, he says. He grew up farming too, and he says the place has always been peaceful and quiet.

Except perhaps for that one period that gave rise to the name Goose Pimple Junction.

Blue Ridge Chronicles

James Gilmer has lived in Goose Pimple Junction all his life.

A Decade of Dispatches from Southwest Virginia

Population sign at Goose Pimple Junction.

The Old Jonesboro Road, running away from Goose Pimple Junction.

The story runs like this: Once upon a time, decades ago, two families who lived in the community were feuding so intensely that they cursed and abused each other with the most vile and profane language they could invent.

A fellow named Bill Morrell quit his job as a driver of a potato chip truck to run a store with his wife, and one of them, after listening to the loudmouthed bickering, said something to the effect that hearing the families curse caused goose bumps, or goose pimples, to rise on the flesh.

Morrell then began calling his grocery the Goose Pimple Junction Store. People began calling the place Goose Pimple Junction.

"It's just a name he gave it, and somehow the name stuck," Gilmer says.

The U.S. Geological Survey began putting the name on its official federal maps after a local resident—a retired USGS employee—petitioned for its inclusion in 1974, says Roger Payne, executive secretary of the U.S. Board of Geographic Names. Payne says the story of the feuding, cursing neighbors is also on file with the federal government.

"These stories are not always true," Payne says, "but there's no question there's a story about a couple of families there shouting obscenities at each other."

Gilmer says he no longer remembers whether the tale is accurate. He only knows that he has heard the account, has called himself a Goose Pimple

Junction resident for decades and recollects that the place was livelier when the store was still open. It closed a couple of decades ago.

Morrell's old store, with its peeling paint and locked doors, still sits at the junction. The junction itself is right in the middle of the kind of gentle and beautiful land that some people can't look at without thinking it could be improved by sticking a golf course on it. Which explains why Goose Pimple Junction is now nearly surrounded by three different golf courses: the Bristol Country Club, the Olde Farm and the Virginian.

With so many greens in the area, it wasn't long before retired business executives moved in, buying up farmland and building big houses with pitched roofs, bay windows and even a few slender, white columns. In between the farms and working-class homes, developers began building neighborhoods of nice homes.

So what began as a quiet farming community is turning into a patchwork of suburbs and tony estates amid golf courses, where duffers speak in hushed tones between putts. You'll no longer hear the kind of cursing that gives storekeepers goose pimples.

Historic Shootout

HILLSVILLE—Carroll County historian Ron Hall will ease himself up out of his chair in the old courthouse and offer to give you a tour of the courtroom where the great shootout occurred, but he won't promise that you'll be impressed. "All we've got left are the two bullet holes in the staircase," he says as he picks up the courtroom key.

The dearth of physical evidence is understandable: Carroll's infamous courthouse gun battle, which pitted members of the local Allen family against law enforcement officials inside a courtroom packed with about 150 people, occurred in 1912.

But though all the blood was wiped away and the fifty or so bullets were gouged out of the walls by souvenir hunters long ago, don't think folks here have forgotten that five people were killed and seven others wounded on that winter day nearly a hundred years ago.

In a rural area where family roots stretch back more than two centuries, memory runs deep. Talk of the shootout, and the resulting executions, can still touch a raw nerve here. Which is why Hillsville residents are now wrestling with a consultant's recommendation that they find a way to exploit the historical shootout to bring in tourists.

To the consultant, who thinks a yearly drama based on the event might lure visitors, the gun battle has the same historical appeal as the 1881 shootout at the OK Corral. To some residents, though, it has the tragic immediacy of the 1999 student massacre at Columbine High School in suburban Denver.

"We have a lot of sensitivities," says Hall, a member of the Carroll County Historical Society who has written a book on the shootout. "A lot of the grandchildren [of those involved] still live in the area."

Even those who support the consultant's idea are cautious. "I guess if it were tastefully done, it might be all right, but it would really have to be

Ron Hall, a member of Carroll County's historical society, sits in the jury box in the courtroom where the famous 1912 courthouse shootout occurred.

tastefully done," says Carroll Commonwealth's Attorney Gregory Goad, who is related to the court clerk who fired the second shot during the gun battle.

The actions that led to the shootout in the courtroom are complex and tangled, but all agree the inciting event was a corn husking in Hillsville in December 1910, where a boy named Wesley Edwards husked a red ear of corn and, by tradition, won the right to kiss a girl of his choosing. Edwards chose a girl with a jealous boyfriend.

A fight ensued at church the following day, and instead of charging the boyfriend and the three friends he brought to help, the local prosecutor charged Edwards and his brother, Sidna, with felonies. The prosecutor was a known enemy of their uncle Floyd Allen, who had stepped in to help raise the boys when their father died.

The two boys fled to North Carolina, but as deputies brought them back, Allen, along with his brother Sidna Allen and nephew Barnett Allen, blocked the road with their horses. Floyd Allen beat the deputy in charge. The Allens were charged with interfering with deputies.

On March 14, 1912, a jury found Floyd Allen guilty, and a judge sentenced him to a year in prison. At that point, Allen supposedly said, "Gentlemen, I ain't a-goin'."

A shot rang out and then another, and soon the courtroom was ablaze with gunfire. Deputies, the prosecutor, the court clerk and the Allens fired

A Decade of Dispatches from Southwest Virginia

The Carroll County Courthouse, where the shootout occurred.

on one another as spectators scrambled for cover. When it was over, the judge, sheriff, prosecutor, a juror and a female witness were dead. Floyd and Sidna Allen were both wounded, as were the clerk, a juror, a deputy and two bystanders. Floyd Allen and his son, Claude, were executed in 1913 after a yearlong, nationwide media frenzy around the shootout.

Howard Kohn, a consultant with the Chesapeake Group Inc., a Baltimore-based firm that helps governments with economic-development projects, says the story is rich with drama. When he first came to study Carroll, he says, he heard the tale so often that at first he thought the shootout was a recent event. He then realized the shootout makes Hillsville unique.

"Counties have to use their assets, things that make them unique, to flourish and prosper," Kohn says. "You have to use what you have."

To others, the shootout is still too recent to bear discussing. Willa Dean Terry, the granddaughter of Sidna Allen, declines to speak about it to reporters. Reporters from around the nation, after all, had maligned her family as lawless mountaineers when in fact they were the wealthiest in Carroll at the time, known largely as successful merchants. The press had also repeated assertions that the Allens had fired first, though the first shot's source has always been debatable.

Terry, speaking through historian Hall, says she does not support a yearly play or reenactment of the shootout because she is convinced it would be inaccurate.

Sidna Allen. *Courtesy of the Carroll County Historical Society.*

Floyd Allen. *Courtesy of the Carroll County Historical Society.*

A Decade of Dispatches from Southwest Virginia

Kohn, though, says a drama could feature multiple versions, letting spectators decide for themselves what happened. He says he'll deliver his final recommendations to the town in several weeks.

Meanwhile, County Administrator Gary Larrowe says he supports the idea of encouraging a private company to use holographic technology and old photos of the shootout's participants to recreate the gun battle. Tourists, he says, would be thrilled to sit in the courtroom as all around them realistic, holographic Allens and deputies shot it out. "If you do not duck when they pull the trigger, then you are not alive," he says.

Today, trials in Carroll take place in a new courthouse. The old courthouse, known as "the shootout courthouse," is now home to the nonprofit historical society and county museum, which sees several hundred visitors pass through a month.

Hall, a member of the historical society's board of trustees, says the society could support some sort of tourist attraction, but, echoing the words of Goad, it would have to be tasteful.

"We've already told the mayor," he says, "we don't want to see a paintball shootout."

Note: So far, officials have not come up with a plan to use the shootout as a tourist attraction.

Diet and Exercise

ELAMSVILLE—Oinky Doodle, Patrick County's most famous junkyard hog, known for his gluttonous love of Tootsie Rolls, Coca-Cola and peanuts, is dead. The big pig was twelve. He also ate York Peppermint Patties.

"A lot of people showed up for his funeral," said a mournful Clyde "Clydie Boy" Turner, who raised the eight-hundred-pound pig at his Elamsville junkyard and recently buried his portly pet behind his house. "I had women I didn't even know hugging me. They said Oinky Doodle's in heaven now."

Oinky Doodle, a pig that state Senator W. Roscoe Reynolds, Democrat from Henry, once referred to as a legend, was only one of the animals that Turner has kept at his junkyard over the years. Other critters included a woolly worm that Turner fed bologna and claimed could predict the weather; a chicken that, like Oinky Doodle, ate Tootsie Rolls from Turner's palm; and a dog that fetched ice cream from a nearby store.

But of all Turner's animals, Oinky Doodle was the biggest, both in frame and name. A Russian razorback that dogs had chased down from the mountains and into Turner's care, he became Turner's boon companion. For more than a decade, the two sat together amid the clutter of Turner's roadside junkyard, and when customers arrived Turner entertained them by offering a bottle of Coca-Cola to Oinky Doodle, who is not known to have ever failed to finish off the entire bottle.

Yesterday, the seventy-one-year-old Turner said one of his prized possessions is a photograph of Governor Mark R. Warner's spokeswoman, Ellen Qualls, holding an upturned bottle of Coca-Cola while Oinky Doodle drank it down.

"Ah, good boar," Qualls said as she recalled the encounter, which she said occurred years ago when she was a reporter for television station WDBJ in Roanoke. "That's troubling that that photo is one of his prized possessions.

Oinky Doodle would roll over to let his owner Clyde "Clydie Boy" Turner of Patrick County scratch his belly. *Courtesy of Bob Brown and the* Richmond Times-Dispatch.

When I was down there, one of his prized possessions was a picture of [U.S. Representative] Virgil Goode with the pig."

Politicians as well as junkyard customers came to know Oinky Doodle over the years because of Turner's role as Democratic ward boss in Patrick, charged with using his folksy charm to prod voters to the polls on Election Day.

Qualls recalled that Turner sang a song for her, accompanying himself on a ukulele, which praised Oinky Doodle's gastronomic gusto. The gist of the song, she said, was that Oinky Doodle adored Coca-Cola and York Peppermint Patties.

"I thought one day we would get to do a Coca-Cola commercial, but I guess it's too late now, ain't it?" Turner said. "He probably drank a thousand Cokes."

Considered a larger-than-life character in the rural county because of his tall tales and reckless youth, Turner credited Oinky Doodle as the true star of countless impromptu junkyard performances.

"At the service, I believe they said he was the most famous pig ever," Turner said. "And I guess I'm a little bit famous too."

A friend, he said, gave him a potbellied pig to help console him over the loss of Oinky Doodle. "I done got him trained to roll over and let me scratch his belly. I call him Little Oinky."

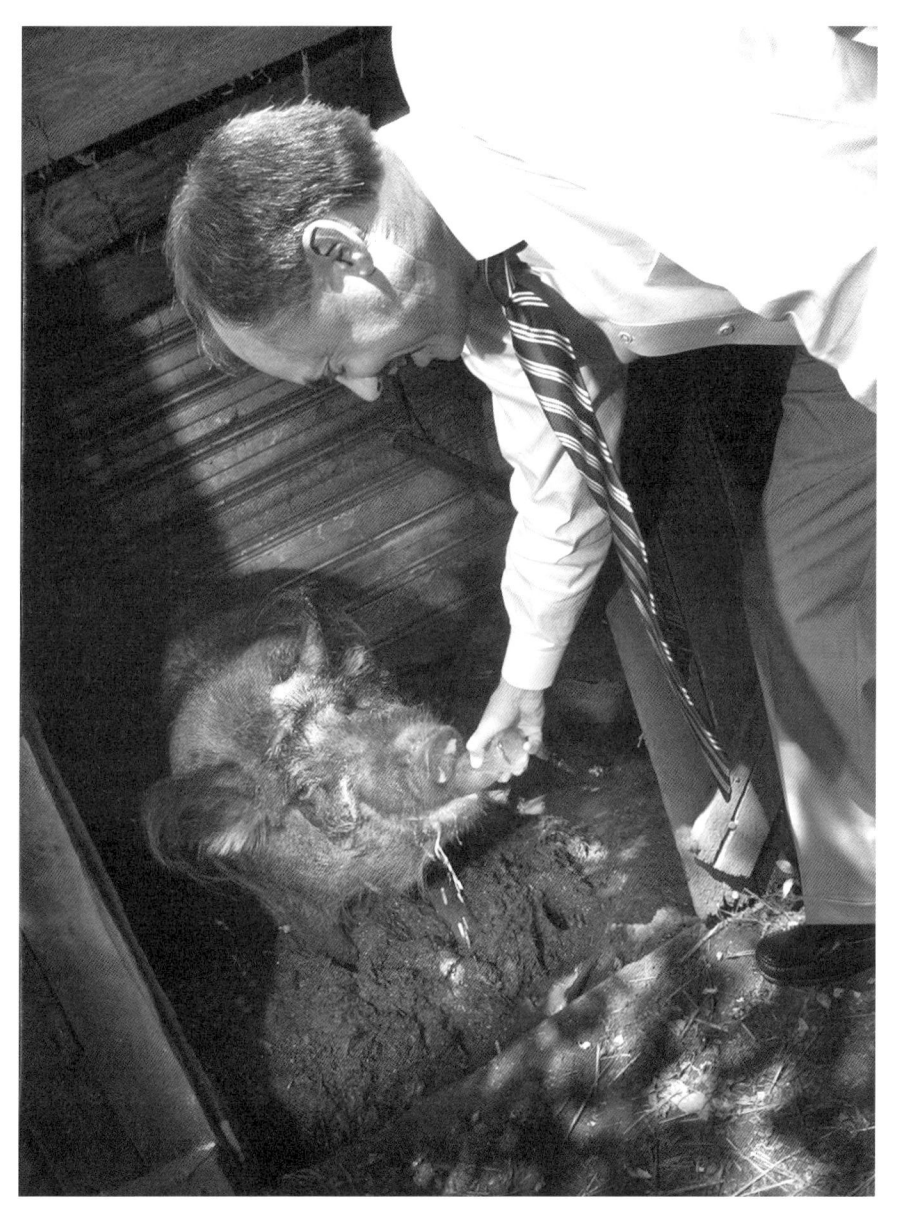

A Decade of Dispatches from Southwest Virginia

Delegate Ward Armstrong, Democrat from Henry, who is now the House Minority Leader, giving Oinky Doodle a coke. *Courtesy of Bob Brown and the* Richmond Times-Dispatch.

Hanging Out

DARWIN—One thing you could formerly count on: When cold, howling weather blew into Appalachia, Stanley's General Store in Darwin became the local hot spot. In particular, the old iron stove inside the store would be the center of popularity in the Dickenson County mountain community. Fired by big lumps of black coal, the stove, a banged-up Buckeye 700 that cost sixty-eight dollars brand new, radiates a warmth that once kept droves of customers lingering—or, as owner Glen Stanley puts it, loafing.

But times change, Stanley opines, and old-fashioned country store loafing is a dying pastime, more popular with the older generation.

"They pass on," Stanley says wistfully. Still, he adds, perking up a bit, "we get our loafers. They come in here to get warm and stay if you keep the fire going."

Yes, people still know the value of a good loaf in Darwin. Though not as numerous as in former times, they loaf around the stove on chilly mornings, they loaf on cold afternoons and they loaf through the long, bitter months of winter, Stanley says.

And with winter on the doorstep and cold weather knocking on the door, Stanley expects an uptick in the number of loafers.

"That old stove is good and warm," says Donnie Dotson, a sixty-five-year-old garbage hauler who says he used to loaf quite a bit at the store but now stops in only once a week to hang out with the few remaining loafers. "The heat from that stove will warm your bones."

Dotson describes the loafing at the general store as "just a bunch of country folk talking."

Stanley's General Store sits at a sharp bend in the road of state Route 72, in a dip at the bottom of several small ridges in western Dickenson. The building, in the center of the small community of Darwin, has housed a store since 1901.

Glen Stanley, owner of Stanley's General Store, stands next to the old stove that draws in customers on cold days.

A Decade of Dispatches from Southwest Virginia

Stanley's General Store in Darwin.

As a young man Stanley worked at the store for seven years, and he bought it in 1970. The owner who sold it to him was also named Stanley, so he didn't have to repaint the name on the sign out front.

"Convenient," says Stanley, a slightly built sixty-three-year-old who wears glasses and a wry smile.

When he bought the store, he also replaced its potbellied stove with the new Buckeye coal burner, which became a magnet for people looking to thaw out and loaf around for a while.

"I'm loafing right now," Stanley notes as he stands several feet from the stove. Nearby, store employee and Stanley's nephew, Nathan Anderson, sits hunched over a computer screen. He looks up from his work just long enough to nod uncritical agreement that, yes, his boss is surely loafing.

The store shelves are stocked with all manner of foodstuff and outdoor gear. There are belts and boots and blankets a short walk from white bread and lunchboxes. The store also sells deli meat and baking supplies, cigarettes and snacks, and the candy bars are within five feet of the glass case that holds rifles and handguns. Plastic bags of milk chocolate crème drops sit in cardboard boxes on the old wooden floor worn smooth by work boots.

The big sign out front says Texaco, but the gas pumps were taken out long ago.

A view inside Stanley's General Store in Darwin.

Stanley says he sees about fifty customers a day, 90 percent of whom he knows by name. The busy time is in the hours after 3:00 p.m., when coal miners end their shift and drop by for supplies on the way home.

"I've always enjoyed it," Stanley says. "I've enjoyed the people, and I've made a decent living at it. Seeing the people day to day, you become great friends with a lot of them. They're more like family than friends."

And every family has its share of loafers.

Metamorphosis

STONEBRUISE—You'll have to forgive Randy Williams if he gets sentimental about the big crumbling house here in the middle of Stonebruise—he grew up hearing stories about how one of his great-grandfathers stored a handmade walnut coffin in an upstairs room.

"My dad said he and the other kids would play in the room and lock each other in to scare each other," Williams recalled before giving a visitor a tour of the roughly two-hundred-year-old home.

The place is now beyond repair. Guinea hens and gray cats roam the overgrown yard. The sad sight of the tumbledown structure stands in unhappy contrast to all the new homes popping up in this Appalachian hamlet. Williams, fifty-one, is probably the perfect guy to talk about the changes going on here in this two-mile-long valley in Russell County. His family has lived here for six generations. That gives him a deep feeling for its beauty and its people. He's also the county commissioner of the revenue. That gives him an appreciation for the benefits of the growth Stonebruise is experiencing.

For Stonebruise is in the middle of a growth spurt. A new subdivision is nearly complete, and Williams expects more to appear soon as aging landowners sell their farmland to developers. County officials are talking about bringing water lines to the community, and that'll make it even easier for builders to raise new neighborhoods. The new homes are worth between $150,000 and $300,000, pumping property tax revenues into the county coffers. The unmarked two-lane road that twists through the valley has been here for two hundred years or so, but it didn't have a name until recently. The county dubbed it Stonebruise Road so rescue crews could better find the addresses of anyone calling 911.

A new Stonebruise is appearing, Williams said, and an old Stonebruise is vanishing. The little country store went out of business about five years ago. Now people have to drive over the ridge into nearby Lebanon to buy a soda

Randy Williams at the old Williams homeplace in Stonebruise.

or cigarettes. Tobacco barns and corncribs are falling into disuse. This is the first year burley tobacco isn't being planted in the valley, he said. Sheep used to graze the hillsides, but they disappeared when the first subdivisions were built two decades ago. "When they brought in the subdivisions, they brought dogs, and that ended the sheep," Williams said.

Construction of a few more subdivisions probably doesn't sound too dramatic to people living in Northern Virginia or the suburbs of Richmond. In places like those, it's hard to look at a vacant piece of land and not figure that someday a developer will put houses or a shopping plaza on it.

But shiny new subdivisions stand out in a place like Stonebruise, where a tiny creek ripples through the valley, red-tailed hawks soar in the sky during the day and hoot owls sing out at night. For generations, Stonebruise has been home to big farming families who fetched their water from mountain springs, raised hogs and cattle, grew corn and tobacco, hunted coons and fed off the blackberries that still grow wild on the hillsides.

According to local lore, Stonebruise got its name because the children who lived in the valley walked barefoot to school along a path so strewn with rocks and pebbles they were never without bruises on their feet. Williams said he remembers a time when the children of the valley played baseball in the meadows or splashed in the shallow creek when they weren't doing chores. Not much ever happened here otherwise. The place was so peaceful and quiet, Williams said, a barn fire was big news. "You could play in the road because there weren't any cars," he said.

Today, of the eighty or so residents, few are children, Williams said. The new homes are occupied by professionals—attorneys, a doctor, a retired plant manager and a stockbroker, for instance—rather than farming families where each child was considered a potential helping hand and even the youngest were familiar with blisters and sweat.

"Every holler had a house in it, and five, six or seven kids came out of every little house to catch the school bus," Williams said. "We sat three to a seat, and sometimes there wasn't room to sit. Our bus was loaded. Now, you'll see the bus go by with just ten kids in it."

But even with the new home construction, you can't say Stonebruise has lost any of its beauty. The hillsides are a hundred shades of green during spring and summer. The brambles and vines are alive with bluebirds. The maple trees turn the slopes bright scarlet during the fall. Residents can step out their doors during the winter and rest their eyes on any number of snow-covered peaks and ridges—among them Clinch Mountain, Beartown Mountain and House and Barn Mountain.

The beauty helps longtime residents stay put. Williams's great-grandfather, the one who kept his coffin upstairs, made a beeline back to Stonebruise

A newer neighborhood in Stonebruise, with Beartown Mountain looming in the background.

after serving in the Civil War. Williams said his own father, who went off to World War II to fight in Africa and Europe, came home to Stonebruise to live the rest of his long life. The war wrecked his nerves—a firecracker would send him diving to the floor—but a midnight drive through the peaceful valley would calm him down, Williams said.

Williams said he doesn't know what the future holds for Stonebruise. "I hate to see all the beautiful and pretty land go into houses. But I know it's important."

Each generation doesn't seem to appreciate the valley's beauty as much as the preceding generation, he said. The old farmhouses are run down and are being used to store hay. Eventually they'll collapse and rot to nothing. Older pioneering families who relied on mountain springs for their water made room for residents who dug wells. Soon those residents will make room for residents who will have their water piped in. And those residents will live in tidy subdivisions in spacious homes where no one would dream of keeping a walnut coffin upstairs.

Life and Death of a Motel

Roanoke—Watching a loved one slowly die is hard, but if the death puts an end to years of suffering, it's a good bet the end is for the best. So say Tom and Doris Wickline of Roanoke. But the husband and wife, both seventy-four, aren't referring to a family member; they're talking about the Parkway Motel, which they built in 1949 and ran for decades.

The old motel, once stately with clean white walls, two long wings and a large cupola, closed in November 2000 after having provided a night's rest to weary motorists and wisecracking traveling salesmen for more than half a century. The motel was once a fixture in Roanoke County, known as the only light on U.S. 220 between Roanoke and Rocky Mount to the south.

Once upon a time, anybody who ran out of gas on the highway in the dead of night had to hike to the motel, bang on the door and ask the Wicklines for help. So common were the late-night knocks that Tom Wickline eventually began keeping a gallon jug of gas in the linen closet of the motel lobby.

But the Wicklines sold the motel in 1973, and for the next quarter century they watched the little business that they built slowly decline into ruin. Owner after owner made a go at the business, but once the Wicklines left, the old girl couldn't breathe on her own. The motel became a temporary shelter for transients, migrant workers, shady characters and the kind of people who constantly look over their shoulder for the law.

The Wicklines watched their motel—the motel in which their son was born and raised—go down right before their eyes. They had to: they live across the street.

"In the past few years, the most frequent car in and out of the motel parking lot belonged to the police department," Tom Wickline said. "There were fights and shootings. It just went downhill."

The Parkway Motel was built in Roanoke County in 1949 on U.S. Route 220. For years it was known as the only light on the road between Roanoke and Rocky Mount to the south.

"It made you feel terrible," interrupted Doris Wickline, sitting in her cozy home across the table from her husband. "It was disgraceful for the whole neighborhood."

The Wicklines could talk for hours about the sad end of their once-glorious motel, but they prefer to remember the good old days. And they had plenty of them. The story of those days begins in Roanoke, where they both grew up. Tom and Doris went to Roanoke's Jefferson High School, but they never met. Their love-at-first-sight moment didn't happen until 1946, when Tom came home from the navy and got hooked up with a blind date. He was an hour late.

"I had already undressed and gone to bed," said Doris, the other half of that blind date. "But my mom told me to get up and go on, and I did."

"And we ended up at the altar," summed up Tom.

Enter Tom Wickline's father, Herbert Alexander Wickline. He was a trucker who created his own freight company, Red Line Inc., to haul goods from Greensboro, North Carolina, to Baltimore. In 1949 he got an itch to make a cross-country trip, and he decided to scratch the itch by buying an Oldsmobile and hitting the road. Weeks later, he came home with an undying passion for motels.

"It was his first real experience in staying in motels," Tom recalled.

A Decade of Dispatches from Southwest Virginia

Acting on a tip that the Blue Ridge Parkway would soon be built to run across U.S. 220, Herbert Wickline sold his trucking business, bought a few acres where he anticipated the parkway would be and built the twenty-room motel. The parkway entrance ended up fifty yards down the road.

Tom was just finishing up at Kenneth's School of Commerce, so he joined his father's new business. He and Doris moved into an upstairs apartment in the motel with their three-year-old daughter, and three years later their son was born in the motel.

"We had a huge living room, bedroom and bath upstairs," Doris said. "And the kids didn't think anything of living in a motel—it's all they knew."

For years the Wicklines did everything. They checked guests in at the counter for four dollars a night, swept the parking lot, trimmed the hedges, washed the windows, made the beds, handed over room keys at midnight and carried suitcases. Rare were the times when at least one of them was not at the motel.

Over the years and despite the hard work, they had loads of fun. Traveling salesmen used to sit in the comfy chairs in the lobby and regale them with tales from the road and other sundry whoppers. Once, the salesmen trooped into Doris's kitchen after Tom challenged one hawker's contention that he could make a tasty apple pie without apples. The salesman proved his point.

And there were the nights when one guest, who stayed at the motel whenever visiting his daughter in Roanoke, played the piano in the Wicklines' apartment. Other guests would leave their rooms to gather around the piano and laugh at his antics, Doris said.

"It was like one big family," Tom said with a sigh. "Some of those traveling salesmen still come and visit us, we got to be such good friends."

The years changed the business, of course. In the motel's heyday—the 1950s and '60s—three maids worked for the Wicklines. The couple made enough money to buy a home and six acres across the highway. Next to the motel they built a restaurant that is still open.

Carpet replaced the tile floors in the guestrooms. Then came coin-operated radios. Then coin-operated televisions. Then free radio. Then free television.

But the Wicklines couldn't keep up. Where once motorists wanted only a wash basin and a place to fall asleep, the big chains, the Marriotts and the Holiday Inns, had given travelers a taste for the extras.

In 1973, the Wicklines called it quits. In the twenty-eight years since, they've seen the motel change hands too many times to count. They've watched the paint peel, the shingles drop and the asphalt parking lot crack.

Tom and Doris Wickline built the Parkway Motel in 1949 and sold it in 1973. They lived across the road from it for years.

And soon, they will watch as bulldozers demolish the motel. A friend of theirs bought it for the last time.

"My father died in 1994, and, in his older years, every time I saw him, he'd ask, 'What's happening at the motel?'" Tom said. "I would always change the subject. And when our friend bought it, I said to him, 'So, you bought the motel.' He said, 'Yes, we're going to tear it down.' I was relieved."

The Cost of a Dam

PHILPOTT—At seventy-two, Elbert Edwards of Franklin County isn't as strong as he once was. But his mind is sharp, and he proudly recalls that it was more than fifty years ago, in the muddy waters of the Smith River, when he began his journey into manhood, using his muscles to reshape the landscape of Virginia. From 4:00 p.m. to midnight, for sixty-five cents an hour, Edwards hauled rocks and swung a pickaxe, working with about four hundred other men to build the Philpott Dam, a 920-foot-long, 220-foot-high structure that created a huge reservoir of water that today appears as a big blue splat on state maps. More importantly, the hydroelectric dam put an end to the floods that for centuries had cursed a large swath of Southside Virginia.

"There was nothing easy about that work at all," Edwards says while relaxing at his Union Hall home. "But it was a job. And it had to be done."

The Philpott Dam is fifty years old this year [2003], and the U.S. Army Corps of Engineers, which built it, is preparing to celebrate.

The corps is trying to track down laborers like Edwards to honor them on September 13 at the Bassett Heritage Festival. Bassett, downstream from the reservoir and dam, has been spared decades of flooding thanks to Edwards and the hundreds of others who poured their sweat into the dam, the corps reckons. But so far, the corps has been able to find only thirty-five of the four hundred dam builders, says Susan Traxel, a park ranger with the corps stationed at Philpott.

"A lot of them are local people," Traxel says of the thirty-five workers she has hunted down. "But they live all over—Georgia, Florida, Maryland, Norfolk and Waynesboro."

Because so many years have gone by, Traxel says she occasionally has found herself talking to widows of the dam builders.

Construction of the Philpott Dam ended years of flooding in Southwest Virginia.

"I've heard a couple of love stories," she says. "One local girl met one of the out-of-towners who came in to build the dam and she caught his eye. She said he used to pick her up at her house and they would tell her parents they were going to the platform to watch concrete being poured—it was being poured twenty-four hours a day, seven days a week and they had a platform set up so people could watch. People would stand mesmerized and stare. So they told her parents they were going to the platform, but they didn't always go to the platform. She said, 'We got away with telling that story quite a bit.'"

Another woman, Traxel says, told stories of dam-building culture. Many of the workers were part of a traveling group of dam builders, the way the woman tells it, and they came to Bassett and surrounding communities and set up their own neighborhoods of trailers, congregating at barbecues and cookouts when they weren't battling the heat and mosquitoes to build the dam.

The Philpott Dam, which straddles the line that divides Franklin and Henry Counties, created a 15-mile-long reservoir with a surface area of 4,060 acres and 100 miles of shoreline. Construction began in 1948, four years after Congress passed the Flood Control Act. The law was passed during World War II to fund dam construction to bring relief to hundreds of communities nationwide that suffered the ravages of periodic flooding.

If anybody needed a dam, the residents along the Smith River in Patrick, Franklin and Henry Counties did. According to corps estimates, communities along the Smith and its tributaries had suffered two hundred floods in the two decades before work began on the dam. Streams with names like Goblintown Creek, Puppy Creek and Buttermilk Branch would swell during heavy rains and inundate the Smith. The Smith would then jump its banks and flood communities like Bassett, Fieldale, Collinsville and Martinsville.

So the corps built the dam, erecting 320,000 cubic yards of concrete from 265,000 barrels of cement and 610,000 tons of crushed stone and sand—enough to build fourteen Washington Monuments.

At least one man was fatally injured during construction, and two others were killed at the quarry that supplied the gravel.

The corps estimates the dam, built for $14 million, has prevented $350 million in flood damages since its completion in October 1953.

To celebrate that achievement, Traxel says, the corps plans to honor the dam builders during a ceremony that begins at 11:00 a.m., September 13 in Bassett. She says the event will include showing old pictures of the construction site that she has tracked down.

Men working on the site in 1948. *Courtesy of the U.S. Army Corps of Engineers.*

This reservoir was created by the Philpott Dam.

From 1:30 p.m. to 4:00 p.m., bands will entertain guests and the corps will offer tours of the dam. (The corps stopped daily tours of the dam immediately after the 9/11 terrorist attacks.)

Edwards, who never saw the dam completed because he left the job to join the Marines and fight in Korea, says he plans to be in Bassett to stand together once more with his fellow laborers. He says they have a right to be proud of their work.

"It was definitely hard work, but that was my first job," he recalls. "That's what put me on my feet."

A Better Maple Syrup

WHITETOP—On a brisk, blue sky morning recently on mile-high White Top Mountain, several good old boys in boots and flannel headed into the woods with cordless power drills and hammers. Minutes later, with a whir and a bang, another maple syrup season had begun.

Cold nights are beginning to yield to warmer days here in the Appalachians, and that's the kind of weather maple sap needs to start flowing. So last week, some of the older residents of the rural community of Whitetop hiked into the Jefferson National Forest, where they drilled holes in maple trees and knocked in plastic taps to catch the sugary juice they are now busily turning into maple syrup.

Though ice still hung on rock outcroppings and pockets of snow covered the wooded slopes, the maples would not wait. And when the maples are ready, so are the old-timers of Whitetop, who work to keep the syrup making tradition alive no matter what the weather brings.

"Hotter 'n a firecracker!" shouted Sonny Buchanan, seventy-four, apropos of nothing, as he hammered a tap into a newly drilled hole in a slender maple. Buchanan shouted the expression nearly every time he wielded his hammer, to the amusement of his colleagues, Buryl Greer, sixty-five, and Jaye Baldwin, sixty, as the men worked their way through a thick maple grove, or sugarbush, on White Top Mountain.

For several decades, the local Mount Rogers Volunteer Fire Department and Rescue Squad, to which Buchanan, Greer and Baldwin belong, has thought of maple syrup as a bringer of life. The volunteer organization uses the money it raises from syrup sales to maintain and fuel its vehicles and purchase new equipment, all to better come to the aid of Whitetop's injured, elderly and infirm.

Rural rescue squads and fire departments across the commonwealth use all sorts of fundraising events to finance their operations, from bake sales to car washes and apple butter festivals, but the volunteers who serve Whitetop (population roughly five hundred) are the only ones to avail themselves of the George Washington and Jefferson National Forests' 1.8 million acres and their maple trees. According to the U.S. Forest Service, the lifesaving outfit holds the sole permit to tap into the national forests' maples.

So it is that at the end of each winter, Greer leads a few hardy volunteers up the slopes of the state's second-highest peak, White Top Mountain (elevation 5,520 feet), to begin another season of making maple syrup. Sometimes the conditions are rough. Last year, they trudged through 8 inches of snow as they set up a new system of rubber hoses to carry the tree sap down the slopes to a 1,400-gallon tank below.

For the most part, it's an affair of gray-haired men. "The young people, they're not interested," Buchanan said. "They don't know about such things."

"People just don't volunteer the way they used to," offered Greer, who said he has made syrup since childhood. "And there aren't that many young people around anymore."

It's maple syrup making time in Whitetop. Jaye Baldwin drills a hole in a maple tree while Buryl Greer prepares to hammer in a tap.

Still, the juice has to be collected over the few weeks of late winter and early spring, when alternating cold nights and warm days work to keep the sap flowing.

Last year, the rescue squad made more than 145 gallons of maple syrup, boiling between 50 and 60 gallons of sap at the community's "sugar house" to get a single gallon of syrup. Each year, squad members sell it at the White Top Mountain Maple Syrup Festival, held the final full weekend of March, charging $12 for a quart, $8 for a pint and $5 for a half-pint. Greer said syrup sales raise between $12,000 and $15,000 a year.

Maple syrup has been one of the community's fundraisers since about 1973. In the first few years, the rescue squad and fire department made some of their own and also resold syrup they had bought from Vermont wholesalers. Unsatisfied with the quality, though, they began selling Highland County syrup alongside their product.

"We thought we could make a better product," Greer said of the decision to abandon Vermont syrup. "And we do."

This year, the volunteers tapped more than twelve hundred trees on roughly ten acres, Greer said, and 75 percent of the syrup sold at the festival will come from White Top Mountain maples. In two years, he said, all of it will be homemade.

When the maple sap boils into syrup, the steam pours out of the Whitetop sugarhouse.

Their system is simple. Holes five-sixteenths of an inch in diameter are drilled in maple trees along a slope, and into each hole a tap is inserted. Small trees have one or two taps, while larger trees have three or even six. A two-foot hose runs from the tap to another hose that runs from tree to tree, always downhill, ending at the 1,400-gallon tank.

The clear liquid that drips from the taps when the temperature tops forty degrees becomes a steady stream by the time it reaches the tank, which is periodically emptied into another tank on the back of a truck.

The truck hauls the full tank five miles down the mountain to a barn-sized sugar house in the community of Whitetop, where Ken Kilby, seventy, runs the sap through an evaporator to boil the water out. The syrup that remains is put in bottles and sold at the festival.

Greer said the volunteers still use some buckets, periodically lugging them down to the tank to empty them, but the system of hoses has cut the workload tremendously. A vacuum pump also speeds the flow of the juice to the tank.

Kilby said it's good that the work requires only a half-dozen volunteers, since youngsters seem more interested in racing cars than in making maple syrup.

"We kid about our younger generation," he said. "We say, if you could put a steering wheel on it, they'd be more interested in doing it. But this manual labor without a steering wheel, they're not into it."

Is This Some Sort of a Joke?

PULASKI—It's so crazy, it just might work. That's the cautious reaction in this industrial mountain town to a local woman's proposal that the entire downtown—with its empty storefronts, struggling businesses and tattered awnings—be completely revamped to resemble a Polish village.

"We've got to do something. It's just a question of determination," said Florence Byrd Stevenson, the seventy-nine-year-old dynamo who has donned a Polish peasant's skirt and shawl on more than a half dozen occasions to lobby town officials, merchants and civic leaders to turn the town of 9,500 residents into a little piece of Poland.

Motorists will surely leave Interstate 81 to drive the three miles into Pulaski to see such a geographic anomaly, Stevenson said, and when they come, dusty cash registers will once again jingle joyfully.

So concerned are town leaders about restoring Pulaski's faded fortunes, they're open to the wild possibility of it all. The town council wants to know if Stevenson's idea is a far-fetched scheme or a brilliant marketing plan.

"She's pursuing this independently, but we certainly want to listen to her," Pulaski Mayor Charles Stewart Jr. said. "I agree full well with her that it helps to have a theme. Whether it would be a Polish theme or not, I don't know. But we want to hear her input."

The way "Flo" Stevenson sees it, the town named for Polish Count Casimir Pulaski can blossom once more with a little paint in pastels and creamy colors, a few flower boxes, a balcony here and there and some nice, tidy trim. Local shops could sell Polish products, and restaurants could serve Polish food. She's talking kielbasa as a cornerstone of commerce.

The fact that Pulaski County was settled predominantly by Scotch-Irish and German settlers who wrested the land away from Indians doesn't bother Stevenson. Turning the town into a Polish village, she said, would

Florence "Flo" Byrd Stevenson, then seventy-nine, donned a Polish peasant's skirt and shawl to lobby the town of Pulaski to remake itself to resemble a Polish village.

be a great way to honor Count Pulaski, a Polish nobleman who heeded Benjamin Franklin's call and fought with General George Washington in the Revolutionary War. Pulaski gave his life for the cause of liberty, in fact, receiving a mortal wound at the Battle of Savannah in 1779.

"We need to bring in money, and there are people going up and down Interstate 81 every day looking for a place to stop and leave their money," Stevenson said. "We just need to overcome our inertia and get going on this."

Pulaski merchants are skeptical, but they, too, are willing to consider almost anything to bring life—customers, that is—back to Main Street.

"I don't think it would hurt if they just wanted to doll the town up," said Tammy Robertson, owner of the Main Street Flower Shop. "I don't see what difference it's going to make. But they've tried everything else, so why not this."

Pulaski sprang up in the 1800s when railroad locomotives began stopping to pick up water. The town then grew and boomed when nearby lead and zinc mines opened, and it continued to thrive with the coming of wood and textile mills. Stewart said he can remember growing up in the 1940s when twenty-seven restaurants and boxcar diners bustled with the din of clattering dishes and chattering customers.

Almost all of that is gone now, though. The last restaurant closed in March 2001, leaving a downtown of old vacant buildings surrounded by a few stores: the flower shop, a furniture store, an optometrist, a pharmacy, an insurance agency and a few lawyers' offices surrounding the courthouse. Even the annual Count Pulaski Day Parade down Main Street has devolved into a flea market–type event in a small park, said George Moore, manager of Carolina Furniture World on West Main.

The town briefly reinvented itself as a mecca for antiques collectors a decade ago, but the antiques shops went out of business one by one, leaving the remaining downtown merchants to watch business migrate a half mile up State Route 99 to a strip of neon-lighted fast-food restaurants, convenience stores, gas stations and shopping plazas.

"I would not want to start a new business downtown," said Moore, who added that he sometimes waits three or four hours for a customer to walk in. "To me, they're going to have to tear some of these old buildings down to make room for parking. If people come down here and they can't find parking, they're not going to come back."

Still, he said, any plan—even one calling for the Polandification of Pulaski—is worth pondering.

Stevenson said the idea is not as far-out as it might seem. She pointed to the little town of Helen, Georgia, to make her point. In 1969, the town

Downtown Pulaski.

in the mountains of north Georgia transformed itself from a bleak row of block structures to a modern alpine village. According to the Helen Society, the 9 businesses that initially agreed to let local carpenters recast them in a wattle-and-daub alpine style have grown to more than 150 import shops and 30 factory outlets.

Stevenson, a world traveler and former dean of women at the University of Tulsa who moved to Pulaski nearly forty years ago because she wanted to live in a small town, has taken her "if they can do it, so can we" proposal to the town council and to civic groups. Next, she said, she will begin writing letters to local merchants, urging them to band together and work to turn Pulaski into a Polish village by 2007, in time for the four hundredth anniversary of the settling of Jamestown. Visitors to Jamestown, she said, will also come to Pulaski—if the town prepares.

"They will come if we tell them we have something to see," she said. "I figure we ought to do this. We just need to visualize it."

Note: The Pulaski Town Council never heeded Stevenson's advice.

Not Fade Away

STAFFORDSVILLE—Wouldn't you know it. Virginia finally decides to put tiny Staffordsville on the official state map just as the community is all but disappearing into the history books. Gone are the general store and motel, the gristmill and tannery, the blacksmith shop and hardware store; they vanished along with the cotton mill and the community's weekly newspaper, the *True Flag*. Gone too are the crank-powered telephones that residents used up until the late 1960s and gone is the switchboard that Elizabeth Eaton kept in her house, operating it twenty-four hours a day with the help of her husband and numerous sons. Even the highway bridge across the Whitley branch of Walker Creek is closed. It's falling apart.

All that remains of the heart of this community in the wooded mountains of Giles County are the little cinder-block post office, where about sixty-five people still pick up their mail; a scattering of houses; a cemetery in the middle of a cow pasture; and a Methodist church named after an eccentric circuit-riding preacher prone to calling down God's wrath on moonshine stills.

But though the community's hubbub and heyday inhabit the past, residents say they are delighted the state map coming out this month features a new speck and the name Staffordsville. And despite the fact that the community has been fading away for decades, they say it as if it's about time the state got around to acknowledging the town's existence.

"I think it's great," said Linda Moye from behind the counter of the post office, where she works when Postmistress Mary T. Gusler is out for the day.

Moye, fifty-eight, said she and her husband have lived here all their lives and have never thought about moving. As she put it, "Well, there's a cemetery up on the hill, and we figure that's where we're going to end up, so no use leaving."

The building to the right was once Staffordsville's general store. The community's post office is still in the smaller building to the left.

Today, about the only sound here is the steady roll of water in the wide creek that runs behind the post office. The scent of honeysuckle fills the air in springtime.

"It's peaceful," said one female resident. "And quiet," added her husband.

Staffordsville is on the north side of Walker Mountain, where state Route 100 crosses Route 660. Pearisburg, the Giles County seat, is a ten-minute drive north.

An Irish immigrant named Ralph Stafford who arrived in this country just in time to fight in the Revolutionary War and get wounded at Yorktown founded the community around 1782, according to the history books. His son, who fought in the War of 1812, set the community on the path of economic prosperity, building a gristmill and sawmill.

Other businesses followed, and soon Staffordsville was a thriving mountain community. Among Staffordsville's most notable residents was the famed Methodist circuit preacher Reverend Robert S. Sheffey (1820–1902), still credited today with setting more sinners straight in Southwest Virginia than just about anyone else. Known for his fastidiousness, love of song and

A Decade of Dispatches from Southwest Virginia

The Sheffey Memorial Methodist Church in Staffordsville.

haste, he was so revered in his time that those who knew him said he could heal the sick and successfully petition God to use rain and falling trees to destroy moonshine stills.

Today, Staffordsville is home to the Sheffey Memorial Methodist Church, a small, wooden structure that sits on a hillside overlooking the creek. The businesses, meanwhile, have all gone — gone elsewhere or gone belly up.

In the mornings, Moye said, traffic along the few narrow roads in Staffordsville becomes heavier as residents head to their jobs at the Volvo plant in nearby Dublin, the Wal-Mart in Pearisburg or the Radford Arsenal in Radford. After the commuters roll by, the rest of the day passes in near silence.

So if tourists are looking for peace and quiet, Moye said, they should come to Staffordsville. It's on the map.

Churches of Rock

WILLIS—Young Bob Childress's fondness for liquor and gambling earned him a reputation as a "heller" here in the rural communities around Buffalo Mountain. Childress once said his earliest memory was of being drunk at Christmas when he was not yet three years old. He spent the first five-dollar bill he earned on a .32-caliber Iver Johnson nickel-plated revolver, he told his biographer, Richard C. Davids.

"He drank," Davids wrote in *The Man Who Moved a Mountain*. "He fought ambush-style, with rocks and pistols. He was scarred from many brawls and twice wounded by gunshot."

But it is not Childress the sinner they remember here in the rugged area where Carroll, Floyd and Patrick Counties meet. They remember the Childress who found religion, Childress the Presbyterian preacher who clothed the poor, visited the sick, sent children to schools, ministered to prisoners and built a scattering of rock churches across the rough-and-tumble Appalachian landscape.

Now, fifty years after his death, the state of Virginia is preparing to remember Reverend Robert "Bob" Childress as well. The state Department of Historic Resources is recommending to two state review boards that the six rock churches Childress built between 1919 and 1954 be added to the National Register of Historic Places and the Virginia Landmarks Register.

The small churches, where mountain folk still worship, stand out in contrast to the brick- and wood-frame churches commonly found in Southwest Virginia.

Randle Brim, a North Carolina writer and researcher who has attended services at all six churches to gather material about Childress and the buildings, said he believes Childress chose to use rock—usually fieldstone—for a good reason. "I think it was his idea to represent the mountain people,"

This church, in Willis, in Floyd County, is one of six Reverend Robert Childress built in mountain communities in Patrick, Carroll and Floyd Counties.

Brim said. "It's the native material and it had a symbolic meaning. It's part of the toughness and rigidity—and I mean that in a positive way—of the mountain people. It represents their strength."

John Kern, director of the historic resources department's Roanoke office, said the rock churches came to the state's attention through Brim. Several years ago, Brim wrote a series of articles on the churches for *Simple Pleasures* magazine. Kern said someone told him of the articles and when he started delving into the history of the buildings, Brim agreed to share his voluminous research records.

Kern said he has no doubt the Virginia State Review Board and Virginia Board of Historic Resources will approve the landmark designations when they meet December 6, [2006], and learn more about Childress's remarkable ministry.

"I call him a cheerful manic," Kern said. "He had incredible energy. And he must have been charismatic."

Childress was born in 1890 and, before his death in 1956, recalled growing up in the mountainous area at a time when lawlessness, shootouts and mayhem seemed to be the natural order of things. Childress admitted to being part of the problem.

A Decade of Dispatches from Southwest Virginia

Reverend Robert "Bob" Childress before his death in 1956. *Courtesy of the Carroll County Historical Society.*

But after attending a Presbyterian church, Childress decided to become a minister. He was thirty when he began high school, riding six miles a day on a mule to get to class with his oldest son, who was in the first grade. He finished in a year and then began attending Davidson College in North Carolina. After a year he quit to begin attending Union Theological Seminary in Richmond.

When Childress returned to the mountains, he began his ministry, driving forty thousand miles a year over narrow mountain roads to preach several times a day, tending to the sick, encouraging the establishment of schools, collecting clothes and donations from bigger churches in Richmond and Roanoke and handing out oranges, raisins and bananas to children at Christmastime. Once he took up a collection of worshippers' pennies, nickels and dimes and gave the money to the convicts at a local labor camp so they could have a Thanksgiving dinner, Brim said.

"He was a person who, whatever was sent to him, he would put it into the ministry," Brim said. "The thing that stands out to me is the way this man brought about not just immediate changes to make life better, but a comprehensive change, a cultural change of the mountain people."

And along the way he built churches, persuading his flocks to gather and contribute stones for the outer walls. "He made it fun," Brim said. "He had contests to try to see who could bring in the prettiest rock. The ones who brought in the biggest and prettiest sort of rock won the contest."

Today, a testament to Childress's work remains not just in the memory of those who knew him, but also in the six churches surrounding Buffalo Mountain: Bluemont, in Patrick, built in 1919; Mayberry, in Patrick, built in 1925; Buffalo Mountain, which straddles Floyd and Carroll, built in 1929; Slate Mountain, which straddles Floyd and Patrick, built in 1932;

The church in Willis was the last one built by Reverend Robert Childress. This is a view of the outer wall of the church.

Dinwiddie, in Carroll, built in 1948; and Willis, in Floyd, built in 1954. Presbyterian congregations still meet in five of the churches. Baptists worship in the one in Willis.

Note: The state did indeed add the rock churches to its list of historic landmarks.

Soul of the Hero

BEDFORD—At last, the valiant men who blessed the shores of Normandy with their blood on D-Day, June 6, 1944, have their memorial. Some of their buddies gathered on a hill in Bedford May 29, 2000, a cold, gray Memorial Day, to remember them. Before a giant arch, three dozen or so D-Day survivors stood, or sat in wheelchairs, to salute their old World War II pals, dead these fifty-six years. The memorial arch is of granite, as if to say: Though their lives were short, our memory of their sacrifice is as enduring as stone.

Representative Robert W. Goodlatte, Republication from the Sixth, said as much when he addressed the six thousand people gathered at the arch's unveiling. "The deeds they accomplished years ago will be remembered by generation after generation."

"A country's soul is its heroes, and it's been said that a country that forgets its heroes will also be forgotten," added Delegate Lacey E. Putney, Independent from Bedford. The monument, he said, "will stand as a constant and lasting remembrance."

Memorial Day is not for the D-Day dead alone, of course. Across the country yesterday, in picnics and parades, in prayers and in the silent placing of American flags in the sod of graves, people honored the valor of those killed in the nation's battles, from the bloodshed of Bunker Hill to the glory that was Gettysburg, from the hills of Iwo Jima to the hot sands of Kuwait.

But in Bedford—which lost more men per capita on D-Day than any other community in the United States, according to historians—paying tribute at the unfinished memorial to those who died at Normandy seemed the proper way to mark the holiday.

The arch looked magnificent. Its polished, rain-washed granite reflected the fluttering flags of the twelve Allied nations that took part in D-Day, the largest coastal invasion in the world's bloody and bellicose history. The crowd hushed when a sculpture was unveiled depicting a dead soldier, his mouth open as if his last breath had just escaped.

Yet it was the frail D-Day survivors, braving chilly winds, who by their presence marked the hilltop as hallowed ground. Where they had once been young and swift enough to outrun bullets across a narrow beach, they now have gray hair and step gingerly. Some complained of aching joints; others leaned on canes or the arms of others. A few carried German shrapnel in their limbs. But surrounded by their wives, children, grandchildren and friends, they served as a potent reminder of what those killed at Normandy had sacrificed: a long and full life.

Several of the survivors addressed the crowd, telling harrowing tales of bombs and bayonets, of seeing friends killed and of killing young German men as they fought from the beach through the hedgerows of France. D-Day veteran Walter Ehlers recounted how he and his brother boarded separate ships in the invasion armada. Ehlers returned. His brother didn't. "That's the last time I saw my brother, when we waved goodbye on the shores at Weymouth," he said.

The National D-Day Memorial in Bedford.

George "Jimmy" Green, once a sublieutenant in the British navy, directed the landing craft that brought thirty-five Bedford soldiers to Omaha Beach, where twenty-one of them soon lay dead.

Green, who traveled from Great Britain for yesterday's dedication, recalled his last moments with Taylor Fellers, leader of the ill-fated Bedford unit, Company A of the 116th Infantry Regiment.

"The sailor always has a great respect for the troops he carries," Green said. "He doesn't always have the chance to say from his heart, 'good luck.' I wished Taylor Fellers and his men good luck, but I never saw Taylor Fellers or his men again."

"On the Other Side"

Bonny Blue—This once-booming coal camp is testament to what can happen when bustle goes bust.

Some Richmonders may have been surprised last week when a University of Virginia study disclosed the capital city's population has shrunk 2.9 percent since 2000. For the few stragglers in Bonny Blue, that's a statistical hiccup.

To see what population decline really means, you have to come to the far western reaches of the state, to Lee County, to Bonny Blue. In the past fifty years, the community outside St. Charles has all but disappeared, its collapse a microcosm of what has been happening throughout Virginia's coalfields for decades as small towns wedded to the fortunes of coal have evaporated and disappeared from state maps.

Few now remember that in the 1930s, when Northern Virginia was a mere backwater and Richmond was surrounded by farm fields, the state's coal counties were thick with people and economic opportunity. One of the counties, Wise, was the second most populous in the state, behind only Pittsylvania.

Bonny Blue, for decades at the center of the economic hubbub that pushed the coalfield population higher, is quiet and still today. Where the Blue Diamond Coal Co. once housed its 1,200 miners in company-owned homes and several packed boardinghouses in the coal camp, there remain but several dozen crumbling homes scattered over the rugged terrain, in deep hollows and along wooded ridges.

Residents long ago said goodbye to the company store, along with the post office, the boardinghouses, the buses and taxis, the company police force, the company doctors and the Bonny Blue elementary school. Gone too is the tennis court that once sat on Big Dude Hill, the neighborhood that

A view from the head of Pot Branch Hollow, in Bonny Blue.

took its name from the fact that its homes were reserved for coal company bigwigs. The coal ran out, and so did the people.

"This has changed so much, you wouldn't think it's the same place," says ninety-three-year-old Velena Rigsby, a tiny, wizened woman who spends her days in her small home in Pot Branch Hollow with her space heater cranked to full blast. "Everybody had a job back then, and things were different. It's a peaceful place now, ain't got no wild people living here."

Pot Branch Hollow is one of the former neighborhoods of Bonny Blue. Essentially, it is a string of small homes along a band of asphalt that quickly turns into two muddy ruts. Dogs, chickens and cats wander across the small yards in front of the houses and along a shallow creek that runs through the hollow. Bits of rusting iron scraps litter the landscape.

"It's real gloomy and desolate down there at this time of the year," says Harold Catron. Catron, a native of Pot Branch Hollow, is one of the many residents who fled Bonny Blue when the coal company started shutting down operations in the 1950s. While other men took their families to Ohio and Michigan looking for work in the auto industry, Catron enlisted in the army.

From there, he joined the state Department of Corrections, where he rose through the ranks until he retired as manager in the department's Inspector

A view from the mouth of Pot Branch Hollow, in Bonny Blue.

BLUE RIDGE CHRONICLES

A dog stands guard outside a home in Pot Branch Hollow, a neighborhood of the former coal camp Bonny Blue.

General's Office. Today he lives in Charlotte Court House in Southside Virginia, where he raised his three kids, and he never considered returning to Bonny Blue or Pot Branch Hollow. "I would have never have wanted to raise those children back there," he says.

Still, Catron recalls the heyday of the community fondly, and last year he wrote a 103-page book of reminiscences titled *Pot Branch Hollow, Bonny Blue and St. Charles*. In the book he recalls waking up to find snow falling through the roof of his house, hauling buckets of water from the creek since the house had no indoor plumbing and helping to dig graves for neighbors who had died.

The book is full of nostalgia for simpler times, for a time when his family made apple butter every year and nearly every family had a small garden plot. But, like the thousands who have left the area over the years, Catron sees no future for Bonny Blue.

He visits family occasionally, he says, and when he's in Bonny Blue he tells people to let the exodus from the area continue. "I say to people, 'Let your children know what's on the other side of the mountain.'"

"A Very Enjoyable Thing"

FLOYD—Getting people to come to Cockram's General Store has never been much trouble. The internationally renowned bluegrass jamborees held at the store every Friday night pack in crowds as tight as a sealed can of salted nuts. When locals in overalls and tourists with cameras jump up on the floorboards to dance to the racing banjo and fiddle tunes, there's not enough room, as they say in these parts, to swing a cat. But if packing the joint is no problem, selling it is proving to be.

"We've got some local people interested, but they can't find the money," said store co-owner Hubert Roberson.

Roberson put Cockram's on the block two months ago. The Friday Nite Jamboree has never made money—everyone gets in free—and Roberson said he and co-owner Freeman Cockram can no longer use the profits of the Floyd Farm Service store next door to subsidize what in twelve years has become the most popular weekly attraction in Southwest Virginia.

Roberson is asking more than $160,000 for the two stores. And whoever buys them doesn't have to keep the jamboree tradition going.

"I'd hope somebody would do it," Roberson said, "but it's not compulsory. I'm not trying to influence them. If they buy it, they can do what they want with it."

The prospect of losing their world-class bluegrass spectacle is as vexing to Floyd residents as any of that rock and roll caterwauling they have in the big cities.

"Many people from the town and the county go there regularly, and people from everywhere else come too," said Ray Batiato, president of the Floyd County Chamber of Commerce and owner of the Stonewall bed-and-breakfast. "It's really been an asset to the town."

Roberson said several people have approached him about buying Cockram's, but no one has clearly stated any intention to keep the jamborees going. One potential buyer is thinking about putting a music store in Cockram's, Roberson said.

"I'd like to see somebody younger with more energy take it over and keep the jamboree going," said Roberson, seventy. "I've had some good times here. But if somebody buys it, it's theirs to do with."

The genesis of the Friday Nite Jamboree has been chronicled by documentary television crews from Germany, Japan and England, as well as by a team from the National Geographic Society. Twelve years ago, Cockram and some of his buddies were in the store picking a few tunes, just practicing, really, when a fellow knocked on the door and asked if he could join. Pull up a chair, they said, and the group started playing regularly on Fridays; soon crowds started showing up.

Today, after the preserve jars and sundry other store items are cleared away, bluegrass bands come to play—without pay—and the crowds swell into the hundreds. On hot summer nights, locals say, as many as 1,200 people attend. When the crowds get too large, the music spills into the Farm Service store, and half a dozen bands play in different parts of the two buildings at the same time.

Somewhere during all the dancing and picking, a plate makes its way around the store, and Roberson and Cockram use whatever crumpled bills

Floyd Country Store—home of the Friday Nite Jamboree. *Courtesy of Fred First.*

are dropped into it to cover expenses. They also sell ice cream, snacks and sixty-nine-cent hot dogs.

"It takes $1,200 a month just to open the doors," Roberson said, "what with the insurance bills, electricity and telephone."

Charging admission is out of the question, he added; once you do that, you have to give the state a cut in the form of an amusement tax and send three dollars per tune to whoever holds the copyright. The only option, he said, is to sell the store and let someone else make a go of it.

Diana Wimmer, the real estate agent trying to sell the property, said the jamborees could continue elsewhere in town if the buyer closes the door at Cockram's on Friday nights.

"A number of people who have talked with me about it said they'd like to see it going on somewhere in town," she said. "It's a very enjoyable thing. No one wants to lose it."

Note: Local businessman Woody Crenshaw eventually bought Cockram's, renamed it the Floyd Country Store and kept the jamboree going. It's more popular than ever.

Where New Year's Is a Blast

Fincastle—Greeting the New Year with a shotgun blast might belong among the more unusual celebratory customs going, but that's the way folks here in Fincastle prefer to do things. For untold decades, possibly for two centuries, this tiny town that once stood on Virginia's wild frontier has said goodbye to the old year and hello to the new by tolling its church bells and firing off a few rounds from the courthouse tower.

They use a shotgun nowadays, but the tradition is so old it might have begun with a musket. Resident Willie Simmons said the custom goes back so far the original celebrants might have climbed into the tower and simply yelled "Bang!"

"It's a very unique rural village tradition," said Mayor Scott Critzer, "but we're not certain how old it is."

"We can't find any old records of when it started," said Dottie Kessler, an eighty-three-year-old Main Street resident who remembers her grandfather, a Simmons, was once the one designated to fire the gun from the courthouse tower. Willie Simmons, her nephew, has been doing it since he inherited the job from his father when he was fourteen or fifteen, and he's now fifty-one. "I haven't hit anyone yet," he noted.

Fincastle, population 359, is the oldest incorporated town in Virginia west of the Blue Ridge Mountains, and even before its official founding in 1772 it served as one of the final points at which westward pioneers could pick up supplies. The town, which sits on several hillocks, is the Botetourt County seat, which explains why the center of town is occupied by an old brick courthouse.

Somewhere back in the town's 234-year history, someone came up with the idea of mixing firearms and pealing bells to mark the New Year, and for all those years since, members of various local families have accepted the

BLUE RIDGE CHRONICLES

Willie Simmons and his son, Hunter, prepare to take part in the town of Fincastle's traditional ceremony to greet the New Year.

charge of ringing the bells of the local churches and firing the gun from the courthouse tower.

The Waids, for instance, have traditionally been in charge of ringing the bells at the Episcopal church, while the Blantons have been in charge of the Baptist belfry and the Campbells have held the honor at the Methodist church. The Simmons family has run New Year's affairs at the courthouse. Simmons's son, Hunter, twenty-one, is the sixth generation of the family to take part in the ceremony. This will mark his fourth or fifth year of ringing the courthouse bell, he said.

The tradition has been preserved by the town's stalwart residents, not its government. "I just stand there and hold my wife's hand until I'm told to kiss her," Critzer said. "And I do."

The ceremony runs like this: At 11:45 p.m. on New Year's Eve, the courthouse bell tolls. Then the Presbyterian bell tolls. Then the Baptist bell. Then the Methodist bell. Then the Episcopal bell. Then the courthouse bell tolls again, and the cycle continues until midnight. At midnight, the courthouse bell tolls twelve times to mark the hour. A bugler in the courthouse steeple blows taps in honor of the old year. This past year, the courthouse bell tolled two times, then ten, then another ten, then seven, to mark the year 2007, Simmons said. Then come three blasts from Simmons's 16-gauge shotgun. All five bells then peal continuously for twelve minutes.

Crowds, sometimes as many as one thousand people, gather in front of the courthouse to hear the gun blast and the ensuing cacophony, though some prefer to congregate at a cemetery behind the Methodist church to listen. In the hours leading up to the ceremony, residents throughout the town make merry at "wait up" parties.

"You hear the bells better when you're in your own home," Kessler said, "so I'll be partying here in my house. We stand on my porch and we can see every bell."

'Shine Town

BUSTHEAD—Folks around this crossroads community called Busthead—yep, it's pronounced "bust head"—will certify that the name is linked to the area's bygone bootlegging business. But that's not the end of the mystery; it's the beginning. There's a part of the story they aren't telling.

Descendants of English and Scotch-Irish pioneers have lived here in the green hills and foggy hollows of western Tazewell County since the 1700s, and one of the grassy dimples in which they built their homes and barns and cattle fences is called Baptist Valley. Busthead sits at the valley's western end. A few small homes constitute the community, along with the ruins of an abandoned grocery store. Exactly when the store went under isn't clear, but the sign still standing out front says a gallon of gas costs $1.19. So whenever it was, it was long ago.

Two narrow ribbons of blacktop—Indian Creek Road and Baptist Valley Road—meet where the store once sat. A small wooded hill looms over the junction. The hill is known as Busthead Mountain. A shallow creek known as Lowe Branch flows beneath the hill.

Seeing the sites in Busthead isn't an all-day affair: Once you see the homes, the store remnants, the creek and the hill that people call a mountain, you've seen all there is. There's no hint that the place was once the center of a thriving trade in untaxed whiskey.

"You get to Busthead, you blink and you're out of Busthead," says Frances McGlothlin, a seventy-year-old widow who lives in a pink house a mile down the road from where the store sat. Her husband was once the store's owner. McGlothlin has lived here all her life, and she says she knows how the community got its name.

The community of Busthead is named after the moonshine brewed there. Busthead Mountain stands in the background.

"It isn't too much of a story," she begins, sitting in a chair on her porch. "A long time ago, there used to be a lot of moonshine sold around here. They called it Busthead because the moonshine would bust your head."

Cecil Monk, who lives on Baptist Valley Road a short walk from the defunct store, confirms the story. He says he's sixty-three years old and has lived here forever.

"They used to make moonshine up there, and they said it was so bad it would bust your head," Monk offers.

The area's corn liquor seems to have been an antidote to aspirin.

McGlothlin and Monk's recollections square with the account found in the definitive history of Tazewell, a book called *Tazewell County* written by Louise Leslie.

The thick book's only mention of Busthead comes in a single paragraph on page 117, where Leslie quotes Busthead resident Jim Bailey, now deceased, as saying the community got its name because the white lightning distilled locally was "guaranteed to bust the head of any man who drank it."

No one here seems to know how long the place has been called Busthead, but McGlothlin says twhe name goes back at least seventy years. Her uncle Charlie Whitaker grew up in the community, she says, and he attended the nearby Richlands High School. He graduated in 1937 or '38, she recalls, and his classmates ribbed him by listing him in the school yearbook as

A Decade of Dispatches from Southwest Virginia

Frances McGlothlin lives a mile outside "downtown" Busthead.

Charlie Busthead Whitaker. That's how she knows the name goes back at least seven decades.

But there's one question residents are less enthusiastic about answering: Who made this moonshine that was so powerful it gave the community its name?

Throughout Virginia's Appalachian hills, probably throughout the state's entire 42,769 square miles, there likely isn't another place named for the reputation of its illicit whiskey making. So which of the community's families deserves the credit? Who, exactly, put this little crook in the road on the map?

"I don't know anything about it," says one local woman before shutting her front door.

"I don't want to talk to you," opines her neighbor.

Apparently, people will chat about lore, but not legal liability. Outsiders, and historians, may never know who brewed the head-splitting hooch that gave the place its name.

As McGlothlin puts it, "I don't know, and I'm not going to tell you."

Old Fiddlers

GALAX—The Old Fiddler's Convention rolls into Galax this week, so once again Oscar Hall is suddenly the man sitting on the biggest secret here in the mountains. Up to 1,900 competitors will pack the city's Felts Park to compete for the title of best fiddler, best banjo picker and best guitarist, and Hall is the man who for forty-two years has appointed the panels of judges who hand out the prizes. This year, as in the past, Hall is keeping the judges' names a closely guarded secret lest anyone try to influence them before the competition or complain to them afterward.

"It's all classified," said the seventy-nine-year-old Hall.

Rumors swirl among city merchants and within the bluegrass community about who might be judging this year, and sundry names come up for consideration; but Hall has become adept at the art of neither confirming nor denying.

"He does usually try to keep quiet about the judges," said Tom Jones, admiringly. Like Hall, Jones is a member of the local Moose Lodge that organizes the event that draws up to fifty thousand people to Galax each August.

The Old Fiddler's Convention is the oldest and biggest event of its kind, begun in 1935 as a Moose Lodge fundraiser. It started as a one-day affair, but its popularity forced organizers to expand it over the years so that it now stretches over six days, from Monday through Saturday. The event turns the tiny patch of Southwest Virginia into the temporary center of the nation's mountain music culture.

Bluegrass musicians and old-time music makers from around the United States flock to Galax (population seven thousand) to compete before a crowd of thousands packed into the grandstands. It's not big prize money that keeps them coming back—the best bluegrass and old-time bands each

BLUE RIDGE CHRONICLES

Channing Russell, twelve, on guitar, Ashley Nale, twelve, on banjo, and Lindsey Nale, nine, on fiddle, all of Galax, warm up before competing as a band in the Galax Old Fiddler's Convention.

Impromptu jam sessions like this one are why many people return year after year to the Galax Old Fiddler's Convention, the oldest and biggest in the nation.

A Decade of Dispatches from Southwest Virginia

Campers arrive on Sunday to find a campsite for the six-day Galax Old Fiddler's Convention.

win $775 while the best overall performer earns just $135—but the prestige of winning first place at amateur bluegrass's premier event.

"There's a lot of good competition at Galax," said Joey Burris, a forty-four-year-old Hillsville resident and banjo player. "I've been competing there since I was about eleven."

Burris said the judges occasionally surprise him but, even if he knew who they were, he would have little room to complain. Burris was declared the clawhammer banjo champ in 1999 and since then has finished in the top ten for seven consecutive years. He came in third last year and said he'll be back again this year, in part because winning at Galax means he can brag to his banjo-picking buddies when he runs into them at other competitions.

Hall has been in charge of the important task of keeping the judging fair and beyond reproach since 1965, putting a three-judge panel in charge of the various bluegrass competitions and another three-judge panel in charge of the old-time competitions. Each judge gives performers a score between one and fifty, and then the three scores are totaled. The highest total wins. Hall doesn't discuss the details of how judges arrive at the scores.

"We just let them judge on the way they play the tune," Hall said. "If they play the best, they win."

The judges—from Virginia and surrounding states, Hall said—are all experts in bluegrass and old-time music, and some compete at Galax in years when they're not judging. Hall said he "keeps a pretty close eye" on the judges, and if one judge's scores are consistently out of line with the other two panelists, that judge likely won't be invited back to judge the following year.

Oscar Hall has been in charge of judge selection for the Galax Old Fiddler's Convention for more than four decades.

As the convention continues throughout the week, Hall said, he relaxes his grip on the judges' names so that some convention-goers and competitors may learn their identities. But hopefully, he said, the names aren't in such wide distribution that the losing competitors can find them in the crowd and grumble about their marks.

"That's why we try to keep it classified," Hall said. "We've had some complaining."

"Gone for a Good While"

BEDFORD—The tramp, tramp, tramp of combat boots on pavement echoed off the brick storefronts of this rural county seat once more March 4, 2004, a reminder to residents here that war demands sacrifice and, sometimes, heartbreak.

About one hundred Virginia National Guard citizen-soldiers, many of them young men who grew up, played ball and chased girls in the hills of western Virginia, marched down the city's Main Street in the cool morning air, striding in step along the first leg of a journey that will soon take them to Afghanistan or Iraq. The last time newly mobilized guardsmen marched through Bedford toward combat, in late winter of 1941, they wore garrison caps and khaki uniforms. The last time they marched through, they were on their way to Nazi-occupied France determined to thump Hitler. The last time they marched through, many of them never returned.

Yesterday, sixty-three years later, crowds lined the streets to wave American flags, cheer and say goodbye to a new generation of guardsmen, among whom marched fifty soldiers from the fabled Company A of the 1st Battalion, 116th Infantry Regiment. The company transformed this community into a national symbol of sacrifice during World War II when nineteen of its men, all from Bedford, died on D-Day, June 6, 1944, as they attempted to storm the beaches of Normandy.

The small city and surrounding county have borne the loss and lived with the memory of the calamity for nearly sixty years, and some residents cried yesterday to see Company A once more march down Main Street.

"They're so young, so young!" exclaimed sixty-three-year-old Bedford resident Doris Stanley as she stood in a parking lot along East Main Street and watched the soldiers in their green camouflage uniforms march by. "I don't know why, but I thought they'd be older. I hope they make it back safely."

Office workers in downtown Bedford look on as National Guardsmen march through town.

Across the nation, Army National Guard members by the tens of thousands are leaving farms, factories and families to join the river of U.S. troops flowing to Iraq and Afghanistan. About 155,000 Army National Guard and Reserve soldiers are now on active duty.

Bedford, where folks know better than most that young men who go off to war do not always come back, decided to say goodbye to the soldiers of Company A, along with about fifty soldiers from the 1st Battalion's companies B, C and HQ, at a public ceremony at the National D-Day Memorial. Leaders of the units, all of which are based in western Virginia, agreed to march the men two miles from the armory through the city to the memorial, which sits on Bedford's highest hill.

The men gathered at the armory, a cavernous brick building on Omaha Beach Circle, before 8:30 a.m., along with wives and children, and some worried out loud that marching through Bedford as their ill-fated Company A predecessors did might be a bad omen. "It's kind of like taking a cruise ship called the *Titanic*," said specialist John Bell of New Castle.

"A few of the guys are thinking, 'Hey, the last guys who did this almost got slaughtered,'" agreed specialist John Krsul of Roanoke, a soldier with Company B.

A Decade of Dispatches from Southwest Virginia

While some of the guardsmen worried about repeating history too closely, their wives fought back tears and spoke only optimistic thoughts.

"I don't feel the danger is the same as it was on D-Day," said Melissa Bugg, wife of Company A First Sergeant David Bugg of Pulaski. "I know it's still dangerous, but hopefully not as dangerous."

Just after 8:30 a.m., sergeants ordered the men into formation outside the armory. Within minutes they set off through town at a march. Some of their wives and children followed them, enduring the lengthy march to remain as close to the soldiers as possible for as long as possible. Among the followers was twelve-year-old Carl Balderston of Bedford County, who kept a close eye on his father, Sergeant James Balderston, as he marched twenty yards ahead. The young and skinny Balderston, marching erect and with his chest puffed out as far as a twelve-year-old's chest can go, admitted he is scared for his father, but said he mostly feels "proud and sad."

"He just kind of said, 'I'm going, and I'm going to be gone for a good while,'" said the twelve-year-old, recalling his father's farewell words.

Shirley McBeraye, sixty-seven, stood on her porch and watched with watery eyes as the guardsmen marched by. She said, "I just hope they come back safe, and Lord be with them."

National Guardsmen gather in Bedford before marching downtown.

Blue Ridge Chronicles

Steele McGonegal, age three, salutes in honor of his dad, Captain Steele McGonegal, a member of the Bedford-based National Guard company.

A Decade of Dispatches from Southwest Virginia

Within minutes, the guardsmen had reached the Bedford Courthouse, where groups of residents, merchants and schoolchildren greeted them with cheers. In 1941, the large brick courthouse housed the National Guard's armory.

Back then, the men of Company A, with orders to report to Fort Meade in Maryland, marched through the city on a bitterly cold night, ending up at the local high school, where they danced. Though it was billed as a farewell event, their accommodations at Fort Meade were not ready, so some of the men slept at the armory the following nights and milled around the city by day. Eventually the army was ready for them, and they took trains and cars to Fort Meade.

After passing the courthouse yesterday as the temperature climbed toward seventy degrees, the guardsmen marched down a hill and past the building that once housed Green's drugstore. It was at the drugstore, which contained a Western Union telegraph machine, that War Department telegrams began arriving one day, weeks after D-Day, informing residents of the disaster that had befallen their sons and husbands. Dead, dead, dead, the telegrams read, one after another, each addressed to a different Bedford family.

The guardsmen marched past the old building without a glance yesterday, turned the corner and headed for the memorial.

At the bottom of the hill where the memorial sits, about six hundred schoolchildren and teachers lined up and greeted the marching troops. The kids screamed, squealed and chanted, "USA! USA! USA!" The guardsmen broke into smiles as they marched up the hill to the memorial.

"This is the good part," sighed D-Day veteran Robert Slaughter of Roanoke, who sat on a bench at the memorial and waited for the soldiers to arrive. "This is the good part now, but when they get over there, separated from their wives and their jobs, it's going to be tough."

Finally at the memorial, the guardsmen stood in formation, in the middle of a crowd of about one thousand, as nine speakers and dignitaries wished them Godspeed. Governor Mark R. Warner urged them to carry the beauty of the surrounding mountains in their hearts, along with the knowledge that their families, their community and their state are behind them. "You go forward with our prayers," Warner said.

The last speaker was Roy Stevens, Bedford native, former Company A soldier and D-Day survivor. His twin brother Ray was killed on Omaha Beach. "You make this old soldier proud," Stevens said in a voice shaky with age. "God be with you. We did it before, and we can do it again."

Following a benediction, the governor shook hands with every guardsman while the Jefferson Forest High School Band played "America the Beautiful."

The soldiers then boarded buses that took them back to the armory. There, they said farewell to their families and boarded buses for Fort Bragg, North Carolina. After several months of training there, they are to become part of the 116th Regiment's 3rd Battalion, serving in either Iraq or Afghanistan.

They do not know when they will be back.

Pickin' Butter Beans

WISE—You might think you'd have to search far and wide to find a banjo plinking intellectual with a working knowledge of marine biology and seasoned expertise in running a college. But you wouldn't. You'd have to look no farther than Wise County, where you'd find Joseph C. "Papa Joe" Smiddy, the eighty-one-year-old chancellor emeritus of the University of Virginia's College at Wise. Smiddy, credited with building the little two-year college into the four-year liberal arts institution it is today, has been retired from administrative work since 1985. But he hasn't eased into lethargy after thirty years as the school's chief: Smiddy and his bluegrass band have recorded a CD of mountain music and bluegrass standards.

Titled *Butter Beans*, the CD features Smiddy's trademark left-handed, claw-hammer banjo style and his smooth mountain twang, which can hit the high notes. Proceeds from sales of the CD go to the UVA's College at Wise Foundation Inc.

Jane Meade-Dean, spokeswoman for the college, said students have listened to "Papa Joe" Smiddy's music for decades—he often sang and played with them in the dormitories while he headed the school—and the lyrics to the songs on the CD are as familiar to many of them as Smiddy's lectures in biology.

"He is a true Renaissance man," Meade-Dean said.

Smiddy is no Johnny-come-lately to mountain music. Over the years he's played with such bluegrass luminaries as Dock Boggs, Randall Hylton and Ricky Skaggs. His group, the Reedy Creek Bluegrass Band, has been performing for more than twenty-five years, entertaining crowds at the Galax Fiddlers Convention, the Dock Boggs Festival and the Virginia-Kentucky Opry.

But Smiddy's musical career began long before his sojourn in the high ivory towers of academia. He was born in Jellico, in east Tennessee, where his father, a coal miner, moved the family specifically so his children could get a musical education.

"My dad was born in 1877, a mountain boy from Tennessee, when there weren't any free schools," Smiddy recalled. "The only school was run by the missionaries for the Congregationalist Church up North, and he loved to go to the school. When he was thirteen, he was pushing coal cars for twenty-five cents a day, but when he could he would go to school. The other kids laughed at him for being so dirty, but he loved learning."

Smiddy's father also loved music. "He liked fun songs, like 'Keep Your Skillet Good and Greasy All the Time,'" Smiddy said. "My mother was a great Puritan. She was always on his case."

His mother's attitude didn't stop his father from moving the entire family—there would eventually be four boys and four girls—to Jellico. There, they were all trained on musical instruments—the mandolin, drums, dulcimer and piano. Smiddy was playing the guitar by age five and the trumpet by age eight. He and his brother Bob, now a retired Baptist preacher living in Midlothian, would eventually play their trumpets at parties and social gatherings.

During the Great Depression, Smiddy labored for twenty cents an hour to pay his way through Lincoln Memorial University in Harrogate, Tennessee. But War World II intervened after two years of college, and Smiddy found himself playing trumpet in an army band at Fort Lee near Hopewell. That didn't last.

"I got patriotic," Smiddy said. "I knew if I had to go home to Jellico and tell them I spent the war playing in a band, they would run me out of town."

So at Smiddy's request, he was transferred to an ordnance unit in the South Pacific, on the island of New Caledonia. Even there, though, his fate was tied to music. "I had to play taps at a lot of funerals. It was always very, very sad."

After the war, Smiddy finished his bachelor's degree in biology at Lincoln and earned a master's degree in biology at Vanderbilt University (then Peabody) in 1952. He began teaching biology at Jonesville High School in Lee County and became principal soon after.

When Clinch Valley College was established as a branch of the University of Virginia in 1954, Dean Sam Crockett talked Smiddy into joining the small faculty as a biology teacher. There, Smiddy said, he found his calling.

"I found something here at the college that I'd been looking for all my life," Smiddy said. "I found thirty-six students who really wanted to learn. And that turned me on to teaching forever."

Within two years, Smiddy was dean of the fledgling school, and the next year, 1957, he was named the director, the school's chief executive officer. In 1968, after the school became a four-year college, he became chancellor, a title he held until his retirement in 1985. Through thirty years of guiding the school, hobnobbing with university presidents and cajoling state legislators for money, he never stopped teaching biology.

Historian Virginius Dabney, in his 1981 book on the University of Virginia, wrote, "A major influence in the development of the institution was exerted by a remarkable man, Joseph C. Smiddy, son of a coal miner who rose to become chancellor of the college."

So influential was Smiddy at the college that today the campus boasts a Smiddy Hall, an endowed professor's chair in Smiddy's name and a diner dubbed Papa Joe's.

Smiddy never gave up his music, though, prompting Dabney to note that Smiddy was also the "guitar-playing leader of the Reedy Creek Boys bluegrass quartet."

Smiddy credited his son, Joe Frank, with leading him to bluegrass. In the early 1960s his son, now a lung specialist at the Holston Valley Medical Center in Kingsport, Tennessee, talked Smiddy into joining his band as a guitar player and then upright bass player. Smiddy played bass for several years, but after three banjo players came and went, Smiddy took up the banjo, no easy task for a left-hander, since the instrument's short fifth string makes it impossible to simply turn the banjo around and play.

"There was a fellow in Dickenson County, a retired coal miner, who made banjos," Smiddy said. "So I took some students and another professor up to his place to see if he would make me a left-handed banjo neck. His name was Darrel Perry, and he had lost a thumb in the mines, but he told my students he had worn it off playing banjo. He said he would make me a neck for eighty-five dollars, and I said that sounded fair. As I was leaving, he asked me what name I wanted him to put on it. I didn't understand, so he told me most people wanted him to put the name Gibson on it. I said, well, I want the name of the guy who made it on it, Perry. He said, 'Mister, you're the first person to tell me to put my name on it.' So I have a unique thing, a Perry, left-handed banjo."

Over the years the band, which Smiddy's daughter Elizabeth also played in before she became a Wise County judge, played at high schools and in front of civic clubs. They eventually became popular enough to play at venues such as Carter's Fold, a large music hall just outside Gate City.

By 1974 they were known as the Reedy Creek Bluegrass Band and in 1976 they recorded a song that Smiddy's son, Joe Frank, wrote, called "Tender Touch Massage." It was an ode to a massage parlor in Kingsport.

"It's an interesting song, but they don't play that on gospel radio," Smiddy said. "And [my son's] wife complains about it when we play it."

Sometime in the mid-1960s, Smiddy heard a group perform a song called "Butter Beans" at a honky-tonk in Atlanta. Set to the music of "Just a Closer Walk With Thee," the tune had the crowd up stomping feet and clapping hands, so Smiddy memorized the words and the band made it their signature song.

"Pretty much everybody in the region knows the lyrics to that one," Meade-Dean said. "It's one of those songs where, when he plays it, everybody claps and sings along."

And that's how "Papa Joe" Smiddy's CD came to be titled *Butter Beans*. Smiddy said he doesn't know if he'll record another—he wants his son to record one first—but he'll keep on playing banjo. "I tell people I'm picking for a living," Smiddy said, "and I'm going to keep on picking as long as my retirement checks last."

About the Author

Rex Bowman is a native of Southwest Virginia who has covered the hills and hollows of the state's Appalachian corner for more than a decade as a reporter for the *Richmond Times-Dispatch*. A graduate of the University of Maryland (summa cum laude, Phi Beta Kappa), he has won numerous journalism prizes, and his work has appeared in *Time* magazine. He is also the author of the novel *Cannibals*. He lives in Roanoke, Virginia.

Visit us at
www. historypress.net